THE BUSINESS OF FREEDOM

MAUREEN ELYSE GILBERT

ISBN: 978-1-7357973-3-5 (Paperback)
ISBN: 978-1-7357973-2-8 (eBook)

Library of Congress Control Number is 2025923548

CONTENTS

For Kayla and Max: I did it all for you!

Why I Left a Six-Figure International Banking Job to Change Beds and Clean Toilets

It's almost midnight.

My kids are nestled next to me in my bed. Some days, after all the busyness at the hotel, it's nice to just cuddle together and reconnect after a long day, their little bodies slowly relaxing in the curve of mine, safe.

Then I hear it. The dreaded sound of the emergency phone ringing.

A hotel guest has called the front desk, which is programmed to ring at my home after hours.

A clogged toilet?

A late arrival locked out of their room?

A bat in their cottage?

It doesn't't matter the *what*—I'm the only *who* getting out of my warm bed to answer the phone. A small part of me thinks screw it. Whatever it is can wait till the morning, right?

That's what I'd like to tell myself, but when it's your business, your life savings, your livelihood on the line, you don't call in sick or pretend you haven't read the email or let it wait till morning. You get out of your warm bed and answer the emergency phone.

None of this was covered in my MBA program. There was no course called "The Unsexy Side of Entrepreneurship." It's moments like these that I sometimes miss my old life, with its expense account and company car. My six weeks of paid vacation. My business trips to interesting international cities. But then I look at the two sleepyheads in my bed. I think of how they accompany me to the hotel each morning, in their own small way participating in our "family" business. Their lives would look a lot different if I hadn't made a life-changing decision eight years ago.

As I pull my pants and shoes on, I remind myself that there are no perfect solutions, just ones that allow us tradeoffs we can live with. I guess my tradeoff involves unclogging a toilet in the middle of the night.

*   *   *

Hard work and unglamorous work weren't new to me. I was a bootstrap kid, and although my family's day-to-day might not have screamed "scarcity," we were far from well-off. From the time I was seven—yes, seven—I learned that if I wanted something, I'd need to earn it myself. I started small: shoveling snow, raking leaves, and walking dogs around the neighborhood. When I couldn't land a typical paper route (too young, they said), I went door-to-door in newly built neighborhoods, signing up fresh subscribers one by one.

By fourteen, I was washing dishes three nights a week in a local greasy spoon. After school, I'd sling my backpack onto the kitchen table and head off to the diner, sweating over stacks of grimy plates until closing time. It was hot, sticky, and about as far from glamorous as you can get—especially at an age when most of my classmates were at the mall or practicing for the next basketball game.

But I quickly discovered that money bought freedom.

Take my high school trip to England and Ireland: a once-in-a-lifetime opportunity—*if* you could afford it. My parents naturally assumed it was out of the question, but when I brought them the permission slip, I told them I already had the funds saved. They let me go because they couldn't argue with my determination or the money I'd earned. Later, when they assumed I'd attend the local parochial high school, I paid the difference in tuition to enroll in a college prep school that would challenge me academically. That taste of choice—the ability to say, *I can do this because I've earned it*—lodged itself deep in my bones and never left.

Looking back, I realize I was just a kid, juggling real labor and financial decisions at an age most people couldn't fathom. But honestly, I don't see myself as special or heroic—just practical. There was no silver spoon on the table, so I started hustling for the next best thing. Those early experiences taught me grit and a ferocious respect for the power of self-reliance. More than anything, they proved that if I wanted to build a life bigger than the small suburb of Philadelphia, I called home, I was responsible for making it happen—and having some cash in my pocket was a critical first step toward that larger world.

The Safe Path Wasn't So Safe After All

Despite my early forays into self-reliance, it was hard to ignore the model I was brought up with. My parents, like many of their generation, had a simple formula for success: go to school, get a stable job, work hard, retire comfortably. It was a path they'd proven could work—at least in their era, when wages went further and corporate loyalty meant something.

Unfortunately, by the time I graduated from college, the U.S. was in another recession, and my economics and Asian studies degree didn't magically unlock a flood of job offers. When the stable, practical path went nowhere, I decided to do something that felt reckless and exhilarating in equal measure: I bought a one-way ticket to Hong Kong.

I knew no one there, had no job prospects, and little more than my optimism and grit to sustain me. For three months, I lived out of my suitcase, couch-surfing well before the term was trendy, living off cheap street food, and knocking on doors in a city whose language and culture I barely understood.

Looking back, I realize that leap—while terrifying—demonstrated a crucial principle I still stand by: *sometimes you have to ignore the chorus of naysayers (or your own doubts) to see what else is possible.* If life has you cornered, sometimes your only option is to break down a wall. Hong Kong was my wall; if I couldn't find a job stateside, why not try the other side of the planet?

Eventually, after countless dead ends, that boldness paid off: I landed a job at a software company, which led to another opportunity, and another. In some ways, that set the tone for the rest of my career.

Fast forward to 2002, after getting an International MBA in France I had landed a job in the world of international banking—a job I'd once have called a dream. On paper, it was perfect: I traveled, worked with global clients, tackled high-stakes decisions, and used my economics background daily. If you had told my younger self that one day I'd give up all that prestige to run a small hotel on the Mendocino Coast, I'd have laughed you out of the room. Wasn't this high-powered gig exactly what I'd worked so hard for—ever since those childhood hustles and that leap of faith in Hong Kong?

Yet, something wasn't right.

The Tension That Changes Everything

I had everything I was supposed to want—prestige, a six-figure salary, international travel—but instead of feeling accomplished, I felt trapped.

My job was the definition of success on paper: I worked with global clients, tackled high-stakes deals, and had a title that carried weight. But as the months ticked by, I found myself restless in meetings, irritated by the bureaucracy, and increasingly aware that my so-called freedom—financial or otherwise—was an illusion.

I had worked so hard to get here, yet I was still at the mercy of someone else's schedule, someone else's approval, someone else's bottom line.

More than anything, I was exhausted by the constant **trade-offs**. The long hours and last-minute business trips meant missing important moments with my husband. I lived in an incredible city—Amsterdam—but only truly lived there on weekends. Even then, I often spent Sunday nights battling that familiar pit in my stomach, knowing another five-day grind was around the corner. Coffee kept me going during the day; wine unwound me at night.

The tension only deepened when I became pregnant. Suddenly, the questions I had been avoiding became **impossible** to ignore.

How was I going to do this?

My days were already long and arduous. I was constantly mentally fatigued. And I knew, deep down, that something had to give.

But what?

I tried to rationalize.

Surely, I could hire a nanny. That had always been the plan—bilingual exposure, professional childcare, the best of both worlds. A practical solution for a woman like me. After all, I had worked too hard to throw away everything I had built—years of studying, climbing, proving myself. The rush of a good deal, the satisfaction of seeing a complex financial strategy come together, the thrill of being excellent at what I did—that wasn't something I could just walk away from.

I loved working. I loved solving problems, making things happen, being in the room where decisions were made. Work had always been a part of my identity, not just a means to a paycheck. My younger self had hustled for every opportunity, and now that I had reached this level of success, shouldn't I hold onto it?

And yet, another part of me—the part that was slowly, quietly growing louder—couldn't bear the thought of missing the most fleeting, irreplaceable years of my child's life.

I imagined the first smile, the first step, the first word—all happening while I was in some corporate meeting, reviewing spreadsheets, or negotiating with clients across time zones. Would a video call with the nanny suffice? Would hurried evenings and weekends feel like enough?

A different kind of ache settled in my chest.

I wasn't afraid of hard work. I had never been afraid of hard work. But what terrified me was the realization that no matter how hard I worked, time was the one currency I could never earn back.

For the first time, my relentless drive—the thing that had always propelled me forward—was at war with something even deeper.

Both desires were real. *Both* mattered.

I didn't want to lose myself. I didn't want to give up the part of me that thrived on creating, contributing, and achieving. But I also knew—without question—that I would regret missing those early years with my child. The weight of that truth settled into my bones.

And yet, I didn't see a way to have both.

One afternoon, I sat in my therapist's office, trying to articulate what felt like a mild depression.

"I don't get it," I admitted. "I have everything I thought I wanted. Why do I feel like I'm failing?"

She looked at me, paused, and then asked one simple question:

"What does your heart really want?"

I didn't even hesitate.

"To mother my child, to live in a beautiful place, and to work in a meaningful way."

The words tumbled out before I could stop them.

Unfiltered truth can be a powerful thing.

And once I said them out loud, I knew there was no going back.

I had been chasing one version of success, but what I really needed wasn't just a career shift—it was a completely different framework for living.

The problem was, I still had no idea how to make that vision a reality.

The Moment Everything Clicked

Two months later—still early in my pregnancy—I found myself on a whitewater rafting trip in Kernville, California, one of my all-time favorite places. As I drifted along a gentle stretch of river, I spotted a small hotel perched on the bank with a makeshift "For Sale" sign dangling from the balcony.

In that instant, everything clicked.

Owning a hotel could allow me to live in a beautiful place and earn an income without being chained to an office desk. I could set my own hours, breastfeed my baby whenever I wanted, and finally have the **freedom** to integrate motherhood and meaningful work on my own terms.

Of course, I had zero clue how to buy a hotel. Sure, I had an MBA, but textbooks don't detail the nitty-gritty of putting together a commercial real estate deal. Still, if my past leaps had taught me anything, it's that lack of knowledge rarely stops me once I commit to an idea.

I contacted a commercial real estate agent to see if this crazy vision was even feasible.

Turns out, with some creative financing, the numbers actually worked. My earlier habit of living on one salary (whenever we had two incomes) and saving or investing the other had built up a decent nest egg. We didn't live lavishly, but we were focused on building a future that could offer security and opportunity—whatever that might look like. Liquidating our retirement accounts carried penalties, yes, but between that and our savings, we had just enough to cover a down payment.

Given my husband's uncertain job prospects, he was on board to take the gamble, too.

And so, in January of 2003—barely blinking at the enormity of it all—we plowed every cent of our life savings into buying a fifteen-room hotel on the Mendocino Coast.

Our daughter was born that June, ushering in a season of life that was equal parts joy, chaos, and total reinvention. I'd traded in boardrooms for ocean views, Excel reports for guest registries, and high heels for muddy boots—and yet the shift felt oddly right.

The dream of mothering my child in a beautiful place while doing meaningful work had transformed from some outlandish notion into our new reality.

And as terrifying as it was to leave corporate safety behind, I finally felt that sense of choice and freedom I'd been craving for so long.

The Unholy Compromise Between Career and Motherhood

The truth is, many of us were told we could have it all—that we could be both successful professionals and amazing moms. Society painted a picture of the modern woman as someone who could excel in the boardroom and still bake the perfect cupcakes for the school bake sale. But for many working moms, this expectation has led to exhaustion, frustration, and an unholy compromise between two aspects of life that feel equally important: career and motherhood.

We've come a long way from the days when women were expected to stay home and manage the household while men went out to work. Today, women can be CEOs, surgeons, entrepreneurs— there's no shortage of possibilities. Yet, despite all this progress, we still don't have the **freedom** that we really need. We're still working within a system designed by and for men, a system that wasn't built to accommodate the needs of working moms who also want to be fully present for their families.

Something's not working.

For so many moms, the reality is that we are constantly torn between work and family, with each demanding more of us than we can give. We want to succeed in our careers, to feel fulfilled by the work we do, and to contribute to our family's financial security. But at the same time, we want to be there for our kids—not just physically, but emotionally, with the time and energy to enjoy the fleeting moments of their childhood.

And yet, when we try to juggle both, we often find ourselves stuck in the middle, feeling like we're failing at everything. We're too exhausted to truly show up at home and stretched too thin to give our best at work. Many of us are burning out, resentful, and questioning how we got here.

It's easy to get trapped in the mindset that "this is just how life is." Maybe we look around at other working moms and assume that if they can manage it, we should be able to, too. Or we feel guilty for wanting something more or different. After all, shouldn't we be grateful for having these opportunities?

But what if you stopped for a moment and acknowledged that **this isn't working?**

What if, instead of pushing through, telling yourself that you should be happy with the status quo, you allowed yourself to feel the discomfort? What if you named it: **My heart isn't happy.**

For many of us, the system we're working within—whether it's a corporate job, a small business, or even staying at home full-time—doesn't leave room for what really matters to us. Our lives have been shaped by the demands of productivity and performance, rather than by what our hearts truly desire. And so we compromise. We choose between being the best mom or the best professional, knowing deep down that **neither choice really feels right**.

This book is about finding a different way—a way to stop making those unholy compromises and start building a life that works for you. It's about **redefining success**, not as how many hours you log at work or how perfectly you manage your household, but as having the **freedom and safety** to live life on your own terms.

It's easy to hear the word business and think, "Hell no—I have no desire or skills to run my own business!" Maybe the idea of entrepreneurship feels overwhelming, risky, or simply not something you've ever wanted for yourself. That's completely understandable. And here's the thing: **you don't have to become an entrepreneur** to benefit from the mindset shift in this book.

This book might surprise you and **change your mind** about what's possible when it comes to financial independence and creating a life on your terms. But even if you remain steadfast in not wanting to run your own business, that's okay. The heart of the **Business of Freedom** isn't just about having a business—it's about **changing how you think about time and money**. It's about understanding that your time is valuable, and that the traditional way of trading hours for dollars isn't the only option.

Whether you choose to run your own business, stay in a job you love, or remain a stay-at-home mom, the key shift is in using your **money even a little bit to generate income**, instead of relying solely on your time and labor. **Money can work for you**—whether through investments, buying or starting your own business, or creating passive income streams like rental real estate —so that you can have more freedom and flexibility in your life. It's not about how many hours you're putting in; it's about creating a financial foundation that supports you, so you're not stuck making those unholy compromises.

The **Business of Freedom** is about taking control of your financial destiny and designing a life that works for you, whether you ever start a business or not. It's about **freedom**, not just from financial stress, but from the idea that you have to choose between being a great mom or being successful.

Freedom: The Real Wealth

Why did you pick up this book?

I'm guessing it's not because you're hoping to remain in a perpetual juggling act of career, motherhood, and sheer exhaustion. Just to clarify, this isn't called *Boss Mom, Burnout Mom*—so I'm not here to offer tips on how to hustle harder or "lean in" until you collapse on the couch every night.

I'm going to assume you're either a mom or planning to be one, and you're craving more **freedom**, **time**, and **financial security**. Does that sound about right?

Let's start with a big question: What excites you about the idea of taking control of your work and your life? What would it feel like to have more flexibility, more say in your schedule, and more confidence in your income? Let's get really clear on what you're hoping will change.

Maybe you're exhausted from juggling a full-time job (or two) while raising kids and trying to keep your sanity intact. If you're here, I'm betting you'd like to shift that balance—so you can focus on what really matters, without sacrificing your livelihood along the way.

Maybe your house feels like it's shrinking by the minute with toys everywhere, and your "office" is whatever room has a lock on the door (hello, bathroom). You dream of a bigger space, but the housing market has gone berserk.

Maybe your kids' school is cutting programs, or your child has unique needs that would thrive with individualized attention—except that private school feels like a far-off fantasy.

Or maybe you're just done with being passed over at work because you have kids. You love your kids, but do they have to derail your career? You find yourself daydreaming about working for yourself or taking a year off just to breathe.

Whatever your reason, one thing is clear: freedom is calling, and more money would give you more freedom to make choices.

More freedom equals more choices.

There's something soul-crushing about being stuck in a job, a lifestyle, or even a relationship that doesn't align with your values or your dreams. Now, I'm not saying freedom means getting everything we want, like a spoiled child at a candy store. But it does mean not being trapped in circumstances that leave you drained and resentful. It means having agency—the ability to make changes in your life when you want to.

And that's what this book is about. It's about creating the kind of freedom that gives you choices—whether that's more time with your kids, the ability to say "no" to work you don't love, or having the financial stability to handle whatever life throws your way.

So, let's talk about that freedom and what you can do to start living life on your terms.

The Life I Didn't Know I Needed

When I bought the hotel, I hadn't yet put a name to what I was truly seeking. But deep down, I was craving **freedom**—the kind that let me nurture my children without sacrificing my own sense of purpose. In owning my own business, I unknowingly created a space where the needs of my family and my own professional ambitions could coexist. It wasn't always easy, but from day one, I felt a surprising *rightness* in being both "Mama" and "Boss" on my own terms.

My daughter Kayla (and eventually Max) came with me to the office most days. They were raised by a village, but not in the cliché sense—this was a community of "Aunties" who watched them while I dashed between reservations, payroll, and kitchen deliveries. Kayla collected eggs in the mornings with Michele, our innkeeper, and helped Karina, our German baker, measure flour for scones. She bumped along in the laundry wagon with Sonia, giggling at every jolt, and wandered the herb garden with Christine, our spa manager, learning which leaves smelled the sweetest. If Kayla needed a snuggle, she could run straight to my office—no commutes, no frantic phone calls to daycare. Watching her grow in this warm, communal setting brought a sense of peace and pride I didn't even know I was missing.

Strangely enough, I also realized the hotel was my *other* baby. As I found myself elbow-deep in the operations—managing reservations, decorating rooms, brainstorming marketing ideas—I felt a creative spark I hadn't experienced in my corporate days. There was something profoundly rewarding about seeing my decisions—big and small—directly influence the inn's success. While I adored my human babies, I discovered I needed my business, too. This enterprise gave me mental stimulation and a canvas for my ambitions, and I was thrilled that I could *be* a mother without muting the part of me that craved professional achievement.

Financially, I was more secure than I'd ever been. Sure, the work was intense—hotels don't close at five o'clock—but the steady cash flow allowed me to invest in three rental properties and buy a lovely home for my family. We took spontaneous weekend trips to San Francisco, and even managed off-season escapes to Hawaii and Belize. We still lived below our means, but that wasn't a sacrifice; it was a conscious choice that let me save for future endeavors. I could enjoy dinners out every week and know that I wasn't spiraling into debt or barely scraping by.

Beyond the financial gains, I felt something even more precious: **time**—time to see my kids grow, time to tuck them in at night, time to share laughter over a fresh batch of scones. As the inn expanded from 15 to 17 rooms, I added a spa and a restaurant and developed nearby vacation rentals. Each new venture strengthened the business and generated enough revenue to support our comfortable lifestyle while still giving me the flexibility to step away. Within three years, I'd doubled the inn's revenue and net income and reduced my own working hours. By 2007, just four years after purchase, the property had appreciated by two million dollars—an incredible milestone for a once-bootstrapped kid from Philadelphia. I could have sold then and become a millionaire at 37 (not exactly dot-com wealth, but still a monumental achievement for me). Most importantly, I did this **without** missing the small but irreplaceable moments in my children's early lives.

Looking back, it all feels surreal: I stumbled onto a For Sale sign and, without a fully formed plan, dove in. But what I found was more than a business; it was a lifestyle that gave me the **freedom and security** to be both an involved mother and a business woman on my own terms. In choosing this path, I uncovered a deeper sense of wholeness than I ever experienced in the corporate grind—and I wouldn't trade that for anything.

Mom's Need Freedom and Safety

Maybe my story won't resonate with you because freedom isn't at the top of your priority list. Maybe you've already found an ideal balance between career and parenting that works for you and your family. And that's wonderful! But there's another layer we all need to consider—vulnerability.

The challenges of balancing work and family often fall hardest on moms, who typically bear the majority of caretaking responsibilities. Traditional work structures—eight- to ten-hour days, five days a week—were not designed with these demands in mind. When a mom has to return to work six weeks after giving birth, for example, she may feel torn between her financial obligations and her baby's need for bonding, all while her own body is still healing.

When we trade our time directly for money, we are inherently more vulnerable than we realize. As much as we plan, life has a way of throwing unexpected changes at us. Sometimes, these changes affect our income or our ability to work, and suddenly, the balance we thought we had begins to shift. It's not just about our own security but about the stability we can offer to our families, especially our children, who depend on us to create a safe, consistent environment.

The mindset shift at the heart of this book is about transforming how we think of money and time. Instead of always trading hours for dollars, it's about finding ways to make our money work *for* us. This shift gives us a safety net when life throws us curveballs, allowing us to adjust our time priorities without sacrificing what we care about. Imagine having financial systems in place that enable you to take time off to care for a sick child, attend an important family event, or pivot toward a new opportunity—without the fear of financial instability.

Think about all the events that can affect our ability to keep up with a work routine: a layoff, a health crisis, a divorce, or an unexpected expense like car repairs or medical bills. Many women are already living paycheck to paycheck, where any disruption can push them into financial hardship. Even those who feel relatively stable may still be just one life event away from a significant setback. And while it's easy to assume these things won't happen to us, the truth is that unexpected shifts happen all the time.

> *Many women are already living paycheck to paycheck, where any disruption can push them into financial hardship.*

The goal of this book is to help you build financial resilience—so that when life changes, you have options. Financial stability for moms isn't just about "getting ahead"—it's about creating a foundation that allows us to adapt when life inevitably shifts. Our kids benefit from this stability too. They're incredibly resilient but also sensitive to the ups and downs in their home environment. The security of knowing that there's a solid foundation in place allows us to be more present and nurturing, especially when times get tough.

In the chapters that follow, I'll share a framework for building both financial safety and personal freedom, what I'll call a Freedom Mindset by creating systems that allow your money to grow and work independently. This isn't about a one-size-fits-all approach to success or wealth. It's about creating a life that aligns with your values and priorities, with the flexibility to adapt when necessary. **My hope is to empower women with tools and strategies to not only achieve balance but to thrive.** Because when we're secure, we have the freedom to be fully present with our children, to handle life's curveballs, and to live in a way that doesn't sacrifice our well-being along the way.

In **Section I: Why a Seat at the Table Isn't Good Enough** we look at the problem many of us are facing. We can't solve a problem unless we can first name it and understand how we got here. I will help you get in touch with how you will be happiest in the work / mom balance. This place of authenticity is an important first step in building a life of freedom and safety. Even if you think you are happy with your balance I encourage you not to skip this section.

In **Section II: The Freedom Mindset Shift,** you will learn the various ways to have your money work for you so you don't have to. This section gives you the building blocks to understand how to redesign a life that works for you.

Section III: Building Your Own Table, will get into the nitty gritty of which path to building financial independence is right for you and will give you the high-level information you need to start exploring options and opportunities. We will look at solopreneurship, starting a business, buying a business and investing in passive income assets and evaluate which option or combination of options is best for you depending on your goals and objectives.

Section IV: You Don't Need an MBA But You Do Need Skills will demystify many financial terms and concepts that are necessary to start navigating your financial freedom in a way that is safe and secure. By the time you finish this section you will have the confidence to start creating your own Business of Freedom.

Let's begin!

Section I:
Why a Seat at the Table
Isn't Good Enough

In 2019, I attended my twenty-year business school reunion at the Institut Européen d'Administration des Affaires, or INSEAD, in France. As I walked through the familiar corridors, memories of my younger self came rushing back—a girl brash and a bit arrogant, if I'm honest, but also filled with a bold certainty that with the right mix of skill and hard work, anything was possible.

I had been invited to give a speech on resilience.
(*Spoiler alert: if you're asked to talk about resilience at a business school, it usually means life hasn't gone according to plan.*)

I'd lost touch with most of my classmates over the years—partly due to geography, but mostly out of embarrassment. While they were climbing the ladders of corporate finance and consulting, I had left the traditional path to buy a business. Since then, I'd sold that business, moved to Indonesia, gotten divorced, and ended up buying a boutique hotel this time in the woods of Washington

State. My resume looked like a patchwork quilt of unconventional choices, sprinkled with notable work gaps and detours I feared others might view as failures.

But it wasn't just pride that haunted me.

I was the first woman in my family to go away to college, the first to build a career, and part of the first generation of women with the legal and social freedom to pursue almost any path. I felt a lingering pressure to do something "noteworthy." Shouldn't I have leveraged my opportunities better? Was I letting down the legacy of women who fought so hard for our place at the table? The pressure to "become something" weighed heavily.

Had I squandered my potential?

What completely surprised me after my talk was how many classmates—especially women—came up to say how inspiring my journey was. Here I was, convinced I was the odd one out, yet I'd touched a nerve. Many of them confided that they, too, felt torn between career ambitions and family life, between achievement and authenticity. I realized that while our generation may have more freedom and choice than ever before, it came with a hidden cost: *constant self-doubt, and a nagging feeling that we're never quite getting it right.*

My great-grandmother, a poor single mom who emigrated from Poland, had none of these choices. She had a hard life—but I'm certain she never lay awake at night debating between studying law or moving to LA to become an actress. She didn't have that luxury—or that burden.

Our freedoms today are, of course, invaluable. But they come with their own complications.

Martha Beck once observed that there are four kinds of women:

- Those who choose full-time motherhood and feel conflicted.
- Those who forego children and focus on careers and feel conflicted.
- Those who try to balance both and feel *really* conflicted.
- And the mystics—those rare women who somehow transcend the conflict entirely.

I don't know about you, but I've never met a mystic.

For the rest of us, the push-and-pull between work and family can feel like a constant battle.

After reconnecting with my classmates and sharing my journey, I was able to see my life differently. What I had long viewed as a scattered path began to take on new shape in the light of hindsight and storytelling.

Each move—leaving a corporate job, buying a small business, freelancing from Bali with my kids, shifting into mortgage brokering, buying another business—had felt like a chaotic pivots at the time.

But now I could see the pattern.

Each choice was part of a deliberate search **a life that didn't fit society's mold, but fiercely fit mine.**

Each time, I was stepping out of a system designed by and for men. A system that didn't offer the flexibility or time freedom I needed to be the kind of mother—or human—I wanted to be. Without fully realizing it, I'd been developing principles and structures to support my life on my own terms.

That's when it hit me:

A seat at the table isn't enough.

Having access to traditional career paths is just the start. What many of us crave isn't just a title, a paycheck, or a place in the room. We want something *beyond* the table—something that lets us live fully, honor our responsibilities, and pursue work that aligns with who we really are.

We need systems that allow us to work with purpose *and* flexibility—to create lives where we don't have to choose between family and fulfillment.

Freedom, in this context, isn't about escape or irresponsibility.

It's about **reimagining what success can look like.**

It's about helping women forge new paths outside the rigid structures that still fail to account for our realities—as caregivers, creators, leaders, and whole people.

It's about moving beyond the checklist of titles and milestones, and toward a life that reflects our values—and evolves as we do.

In that room, surrounded by people I once measured myself against, I realized I had a story worth telling. The decisions that once felt like deviations were actually declarations of freedom. And if I could help other women do the same—build lives that support their most essential goals *without sacrificing themselves in the process* **...then that would be a legacy worth leaving.**

So here we are.

No longer content with a seat at the table.
We're daring to build a new one altogether.

One where our choices aren't bound by outdated structures.
One where work, family, and purpose can coexist.
One where every woman has the freedom—and the financial power—to shape her life with intention and courage.

CHAPTER 1

What Women Want

Lady Ragnell

There is a tale in the *Legend of King Arthur and the Knights of the Round Table* known as "The Loathsome Lady." The legend goes that one-day King Arthur killed a magnificent stag in the woods belonging to one of his sworn enemies, Sir Gromer. Separated from his men and out of arrows, Arthur was about to be slain by Sir Gromer but instead was offered a chance to live if he could answer a riddle: What do women desire most, above all else?

Arthur vowed to return in a year and a day with the correct answer—or else submit to his fate. He enlisted the help of his young, noble-hearted nephew, Sir Gawain, to travel the kingdom in search of the truth. Together, they questioned women from all walks of life, but every answer was different.

Some said women most desired to be adorned in fine clothes. Others longed for a life of comfort and ease. A few claimed women wanted strong, handsome husbands. But no matter how many they asked, no clear answer emerged.

As the months passed, their hope dimmed. With only a month remaining, they returned to court empty-handed, disheartened and no closer to solving the riddle.

One day, while riding alone through the woods near Camelot, King Arthur's horse reared back in fright at a ghastly figure standing by the path. Before him stood a woman—shriveled and stooped, her face marked with sores, her nose hooked like a bird's beak. Arthur had never seen a creature so repulsive.

And yet, the woman spoke with clarity and certainty. She claimed that *she alone* knew the answer to his riddle. But there was a price: in exchange for the truth, Arthur must promise her the hand of his noble nephew, Sir Gawain.

Desperate and out of options, Arthur agreed.

The woman then spoke the words that would change everything:

> *"What women desire above all else is sovereignty—*
> *to rule our own lives, to act according to our will,*
> *and to be beholden to no one."*

Arthur rode back to court and presented the answer. To his immense relief, it was correct—and his life was spared.

True to his word, he arranged the wedding of Sir Gawain and the loathsome lady for the very next day.

It is a testament to Sir Gawain's honor and loyalty that he did not flee when he saw his bride at the altar. She was, by all accounts, the most wretched and grotesque creature he had ever laid eyes on. And to make matters worse, she insisted they consummate the marriage without delay.

But when they retired to the wedding chamber, Gawain was stunned. Before him stood not the hideous figure he had wed, but the most radiant woman he had ever seen.

Overcome with astonishment—and not a little eagerness—he moved toward her. But she held up a hand.

She explained that she had been cursed years ago by her brother – none other than the fearsome Sir Gromer. The enchantment condemned her to take the form of a loathsome creature, except for brief periods when her true self could emerge.

Gawain had a choice: she could appear in her natural, beautiful form by night, when they were alone… or by day, when others would see her. But not both.

For a young man, it was no small dilemma — the allure of a beautiful wife in private weighed against the scorn or pity he might endure in public, or the reverse.

Despite the inner grappling, Sir Gawain, gallant and wise, did not hesitate.

He said, "The choice is not mine to make. It is yours. I will honor whatever you choose for yourself." At this, his bride wept—not from sorrow, but relief.

For that was the very condition required to break the spell: that a man, of his own free will, would grant her the sovereignty to decide her own fate.

From that moment on, the enchantment was broken. She remained in her true form, both day and night. And as the tale goes, they lived happily ever after.

Freedom of Choice

While we no longer live in a time of knights and ladies and arranged marriages, it wasn't all that long ago that women lacked even the most basic financial autonomy.

- In the UK, a woman couldn't open a bank account or apply for a loan without her father's signature—even if she earned more than him—until 1975.
- In the U.S., it wasn't until 1974, with the passing of the Equal Credit Opportunity Act, that women could get their own credit cards.

Both of these milestones happened after I was born.

If you've never looked up the "timeline of women's rights," I encourage you to do it. It's a stark reminder of just how recently women began gaining sovereignty over their own lives. We've come a long way, baby... *or have we?*

If you're part of Generation X, like me, you were probably raised to believe that *not* taking full advantage of these hard-won rights—especially the right to "have it all"—was somehow letting down your gender. And yet, if you've ever found yourself wondering whether these freedoms have made us *happier*—or just more overworked and depleted—you're not alone.

When I was newly divorced and just beginning to contemplate the dating scene, the thought of getting dressed up, going out, and "being on" felt like a full-time job. Staying home in pajamas with a good book sounded infinitely better. And then it hit me:

I didn't need a new husband. I needed a wife.

Of course, I immediately scolded myself for having such a gender-stereotypical, heteronormative thought—especially since all I'd be doing was transferring my unbearable workload to another poor woman.

What I really needed was a team.

I needed a cook. A housecleaner. A nanny. A chauffeur. A handyperson who could do minor repairs. And ideally, someone who could also contribute to the family finances.

At first, I thought these were just the woes of a single working mom. But the more I talked to women—married, divorced, partnered, or solo—the more I heard the same thing:

We are expected to be *on*, performing, producing, and caretaking from the moment our feet hit the floor to the moment we collapse into bed.

I'm not suggesting we go back to a time when women lacked choice. Of course not.

But something about this version of freedom—the one we've inherited—**isn't working.**

Finding Authenticity

Women can be our own worst enemies—not because we're flawed, but because we've been conditioned to over function. The exhaustion so many of us feel doesn't always come from the demands of others. More often, it comes from trying to be all things to all people—performing roles that don't fully align with who we truly are.

Instead of living from a place of authenticity, we push ourselves to meet expectations that were never ours to begin with.

This is why I care so deeply about helping women change their relationship with money—not because wealth is the goal, but because **freedom** is. Freedom to show up as the most honest, aligned version of ourselves. Freedom to stop performing. Freedom to choose.

I've always loved the etymology of words—they carry buried truths. *Authenticity* comes from the Greek word *authentes*, meaning "one acting of their own authority." That's the heart of it. Like Lady Ragnell, what women want—what we *need*—is sovereignty: the safety and power to live life on our own terms.

And that will look different for every woman.

Your version of success doesn't have to match anyone else's. Your choices don't need to be impressive—they need to be **true**.

- Maybe you showed up to the school bake sale with store-bought cupcakes full of gluten, peanuts, and red dye number 40 because you forgot it was bake sale day. That doesn't mean you're failing.

- Maybe you're at a cocktail party and feel sheepish saying you're a stay-at-home mom—or that you work a hybrid job that fits your life but doesn't impress anyone. That doesn't make your path lesser.

We *can* have it all—but not everything, everywhere, all at once. The real question is: **what does "having it all" mean to *you*?** And how do you structure your life, your time, and yes—your money— to honor that vision?

When we free ourselves from the pressure to meet externally defined ideals, money becomes something else entirely. Not a chase. Not a measurement of worth. But a tool to build a life that fits. A life that feels like our own.

But we can't do that until we give ourselves permission to *be* who we are—fully, unapologetically, and on purpose.

So let's begin by exploring the three most common ways women approach this journey to authenticity…

Super Moms and Boss Bitches

When a woman today decides to become a mother, she effectively has three choices:

1. Pause her career or income earning and stay at home as primary caretaker to the children
2. Focus on her career and income earning and outsource the primary caretaking to someone else
3. Hobble together an unholy balance between caretaking and income earning

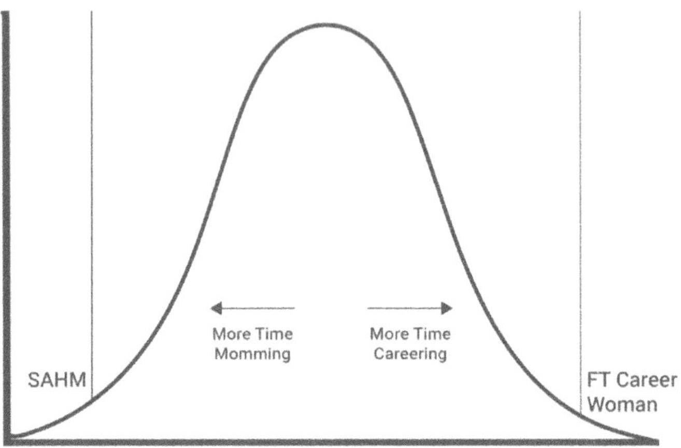

For the moment, I'm going to assume that women who choose to be stay-at-home moms (SAHMs) or full-time caretakers are doing so because, in their hearts, it brings them the most fulfillment—and because they can financially afford to make that choice. Likewise, I'll assume that women who primarily focus on their careers and outsource childcare are doing so not because they love their children any less, but because stepping away from their professional path would feel like a loss of purpose and self.

In both cases, fully embracing either caretaking or career is a valid and empowering choice.

Take Stephanie, a top doctor at Stanford Hospital. She's known she wanted to be a doctor since childhood. Her work gives her deep meaning and purpose. She also loves her kids—but she finds the daily tasks of caretaking small children mind-numbing. Singing songs on repeat and endless playground visits just aren't her thing. Luckily, she has a nanny who has been with her family for years.

"She is a godsend. The kids adore her, and she's great at all the things I'm not. If I were home full-time, I'd probably resent my kids—and no child deserves to feel that. Because I love my job, the time I do spend with them is all the more precious."

By contrast, Meghan always dreamed of being a mom. Her partner has a stable, well-paying job, and values the time and energy Meghan puts into being the "CEO of the family." They're financially comfortable on one salary, and every time she considers returning to work, it becomes clear that doing so would actually *reduce* her family's freedom—not expand it.

"When I think about everything I'd have to outsource— childcare, meal prep, the endless logistics—we'd actually be less well off financially. And honestly? I like being the primary parent, and my partner sees the value in that."

These women live on opposite ends of the spectrum, yet they share one crucial thing: **they're happy with their choices**. Neither feels deprived or secretly longs for the other path. Maybe you identify with one of them.

But what if you don't? Then my friend you are stuck in the middle.

Stuck in the Middle – The Real Struggle

That leaves the rest of us: the ones in the messy middle. We have mixed desires and needs when it comes to how much time we want—or need—to devote to both work and caretaking.

Would a four-day workweek give you breathing room?

Would working from home help you better interweave your mom life and professional life?

Would a creative project or part-time mission-driven work feel more fulfilling than either a traditional job or full-time parenting?

If you're stuck in the middle, you're not alone.

And more importantly: you're not broken.

You're simply someone who needs *more flexibility*, more *agency*, and perhaps more *income* to redesign your life in a way that doesn't compromise your financial stability or your soul.

The first step in adopting a freedom mindset is recognizing that you live in this middle zone—and that creating a better balance may require a path beyond what traditional jobs tend to offer. There's enormous freedom in simply admitting that the status quo isn't working for you. You don't need to fit neatly into the box of full-time mom or full-time employee.

In fact, giving yourself permission to want *something else*—whether that's a reimagined schedule, a hybrid setup, or a completely new venture—might be the most powerful move you make.

So start by honoring your truth: if the current balance isn't working, say so. Then let that honesty guide you.

The rest of this book will help you take the next step—not just with inspiration, but with practical tools and strategies to make your version of freedom real.

The truth is, you don't want it all.

You want *your* all.

And by picking up this book, you've already had the courage to say:

There must be another way.

You weren't wrong.

You were just missing the roadmap.

What If You've Already Found Freedom?

Maybe you're reading this and thinking,

"Actually, I like the balance I've created. My work-life mix works for me."

If so—that's amazing. Truly.

But there's one more piece we can't afford to overlook: **security.**

Because **the freedom mindset isn't just about choice—it's also about safety.**

You may have time freedom now. You may love your flexible schedule, your hybrid setup, or the ability to prioritize your family without burning out.

But can you sustain it?

Because real freedom isn't just about having choices today. It's about having a *safety net for tomorrow.*

Take Stephanie and Meghan from earlier:

Stephanie has a job she loves and a fabulous nanny.

Meghan relies on her partner's income and focuses on raising their kids.

Both have found a rhythm that works *for now*—but what happens if life throws a curveball?

What if Meghan's partner loses his job—or his life insurance wasn't enough?

What if Stephanie is laid off or loses her nanny?

What if either of them faces a major medical crisis or unexpected financial burden?

As long as their income—or the income they rely on—is tied to *trading time for money,* their freedom is vulnerable.

And that's what this book is here to help you change.

Not by piling on more to-dos. Not by scaring you into scarcity.

But by showing you how to build a structure for your life that offers **both** time freedom *and* income resilience.

So before we go any further, let's take a look at where *you* are right now on the work/mom curve—and what freedom means for *your* season of life.

Exercise: Where Are You—And Where Do You Long to Be?

I believe we all have a quiet, wise voice inside us that knows our deepest truths. Even if our mind rushes in with a thousand *"yes, but…"* objections, that inner voice holds the key to our happiness.

Some women access it through stillness and silence. For me, it often arrives when I'm walking. Whatever helps you drop out of your head and into your body—*do that now.*

Then, take a look at the bell curve below. It reflects a spectrum from full-time caretaking on one end to full-time working on the other.

First, mark where you are now.

Where on the curve do you actually live?

Then, ask yourself—if money weren't a factor, where on the spectrum would you *want* to be?

Would you spend more time with your kids?

More time on work that fuels you?

Would you shift the balance to give more time to a creative project, your community, or even rest?

How big is the gap between where you are *now* and where you want to be?

If it's small—wonderful. You're already close.

If it's large—don't panic. That gap is the fuel.

It's your invitation to begin.

This book exists to help you bridge that gap—with clarity, with courage, and with a plan that fits *you*.

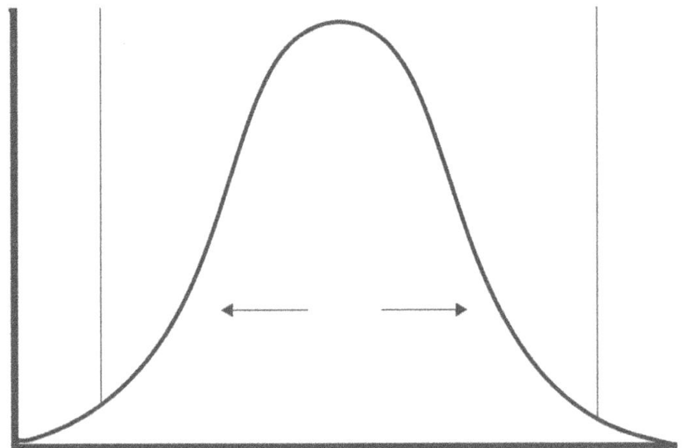

CHAPTER 2

How We Get Stuck

No one wakes up and says, *"Today's the day I'm going to make a series of decisions that will leave me trapped in a situation I hate, unable to break free."* Believe me, I didn't. And yet, three times in my life, I found myself in exactly that position—feeling the deep frustration of not having the financial means or security to live the life I envisioned.

When we feel stuck, it's easy to blame ourselves. We wonder if we made the wrong choices, if we didn't try hard enough, or if we simply don't deserve better. But here's the truth: there are real, powerful forces at work in our lives that we often overlook. Forces that impact us more than we realize and that keep us locked in patterns we can't easily escape.

Before we can fix a problem, we have to name it and understand how we got there otherwise the solution won't fit the problem. We will look at how three factors: lifestyle leverage; time scarcity and unexpected life events can cause us to have to confront what isn't working in our lives.

Financial Bondage 101

Many of us follow a path that feels so ingrained, we rarely stop to question it: we finish our education, find a job, and start earning. Our income becomes the primary tool to construct our lifestyle. The first step is often moving out of our parents' house and finding a place of our own. Next, we might buy a car, or upgrade to a newer model if we're already driving. Over time, as we earn raises or switch jobs for higher-paying positions, we use the additional income to fund further lifestyle upgrades—maybe a nicer apartment, a home, a better car, or even designer clothing and luxury goods.

What we often don't realize is that, with every upgrade, we dig ourselves deeper into a financial cycle. Our income and lifestyle are locked in a dance—our spending grows with our earnings, and we become dependent on that higher income to maintain the lifestyle we've built. But here's the kicker: when our lifestyle inflates, so does our need to earn more. The result? We become trapped in a cycle of working harder to fund the very life we thought would make us happy.

This cycle creates a form of **financial bondage**. Instead of our finances serving us—enabling us to live on our terms—our lifestyle starts demanding that we keep earning at the same or higher levels. We become *slaves to our income*. The more we upgrade, the harder it becomes to step off the treadmill.

When maintaining our lifestyle becomes our priority, we lose sight of the freedom and happiness we were originally seeking. Financial decisions no longer revolve around our values, passions, or desires—they revolve around *maintaining a life we've been taught to want*. The trap closes in: high-paying jobs, long hours, and little room to pivot or take risks—whether it's switching careers, starting a business, or scaling back on work to spend time on other pursuits.

The path to **real financial independence** feels elusive.

Time Scarcity: The Silent Limit

There are only so many hours in a day and days in a year.

As long as you're trading your time for money, you will always have a cap on how much you can make. Even if you take on two or three jobs, you are still constrained by the limits of time. This time scarcity creates a ceiling on your income potential, making it impossible to earn beyond a certain point no matter how hard you work.

The true weight of time scarcity doesn't hit until life starts demanding more of both your time and your money. Whether it's starting a family, going back to school, or caring for aging parents, these changes bring not just financial pressure but also consume the very time you need to meet those demands. These life shifts often require significant financial outlays—childcare, healthcare, tuition—and at the same time, they reduce the hours available to earn the income needed to support them.

Take starting a family, for example. The financial burden is clear, but so is the time commitment. Childcare, healthcare, and education require money, while parenting demands your time, leaving less of it to work. Similarly, returning to school might offer the potential for future earnings growth, but in the short term, it adds expenses and reduces the hours you can commit to paid work.

The irony is that these life-changing decisions, which could enrich your future, often end up feeling like burdens. Time scarcity limits your ability to balance both the growing financial demands and your shrinking time.

In this way, many of us find ourselves trapped between two constraints: time and money. With no more hours to trade for income and rising life costs, it can feel like no matter how hard we work, it's never enough. This is the cycle of trading time for money—always running but never getting ahead. Until we break this connection, the pressures of life continue to compound, making it harder to feel both financially and personally free.

Shit Happens: The Curveballs Life Throws

No matter how carefully you plan or how balanced your financial life seems, life can throw unexpected challenges your way. Sometimes, it's a sudden change—a surprise pregnancy, a partner leaving, or losing a job—that disrupts everything. These "shit happens" moments can make even a stable financial situation feel precarious. And when your income is tied directly to your time, these events can trap you in a situation where your money no longer works for you.

When these unexpected moments arise, you may suddenly find yourself with more financial demands—medical bills, childcare costs, or the need to cover living expenses while you search for a new job. Yet, at the same time, your ability to work, and therefore earn, may become more limited. If you've been trading time for money, this creates an impossible dilemma: your financial needs increase, but the time you can devote to earning that money shrinks.

The balance you once had between income and expenses is thrown off, and you may feel stuck, scrambling to maintain the lifestyle you've built or simply make ends meet. The more you try to solve this by working harder or taking on more hours, the deeper you get trapped in the cycle of trading time for money. And, when life demands more time from you—whether it's caring for a new child, navigating the emotional fallout of a breakup, or job hunting— there's simply no more time to give.

The Gift of Tension

Whether lifestyle has slowly crept up on you to the point that you feel trapped; or you're beginning to realize the reality of time scarcity or you've been confronted by a shit happens life event that you weren't prepared for you are probably feeling **tension**. If so then congratulations. I realize that this might not feel like a moment to celebrate but tension is actually your friend.

Tension is that little voice inside telling you something in your life is out of balance. Many of us are so conditioned by societal expectations and norms—"this is what life is supposed to be"— that we've learned to ignore or suppress those inner tugs that say, "I'm unhappy," or, "Something isn't right." We dismiss them as fleeting frustrations or chalk them up to stress, rather than pausing to consider what that discomfort might be trying to tell us.

But what if the tension you feel is not something to brush aside, but your authentic self trying to get your attention? That inner unease is often a sign that you're misaligned in some area of your life—whether it's the way you're spending your time, the career path you're on, or the financial choices you're making. Tension is your inner compass telling you that somewhere, something is not in harmony with your true values or desires.

This kind of tension often arises when there's a disconnect between what we think we should be doing and what our deeper self truly wants. We push forward, following the prescribed steps society has laid out—working hard, chasing higher pay, acquiring more—but underneath it all, our true selves are quietly protesting. The discomfort that bubbles up isn't just dissatisfaction; it's your inner voice trying to communicate that something needs to change.

We often see tension as something negative, something to be avoided or minimized. But in reality, tension is a guide. It's your authentic self saying, "Pay attention. You are out of alignment." Instead of dismissing it, what if we used it as a tool to explore what's really going on beneath the surface? What if the key to resolving that tension lies in understanding where your life and your values have drifted apart?

By learning to listen to the tension rather than fight it, you can begin to identify where you're out of sync with your true self. It's an invitation to explore deeper questions: What am I really seeking? What parts of my life no longer serve me? What adjustments do I need to make to realign with my authentic desires?

Real World Women, Real Problems

It's easy to dismiss what isn't working in our lives when we've been conditioned to believe that, compared to the real suffering in the world, our problems are insignificant. We tell ourselves, "I shouldn't complain—I have it so good compared to others," or "This is just a first world problem." And while it's true that many of us live in relative comfort compared to those facing extreme hardship, that doesn't mean the tension we feel in our own lives isn't real or worth addressing.

This mindset often leads us to minimize our own struggles, pushing down feelings of dissatisfaction or stress because we think we don't have the right to feel that way. But ignoring these inner tugs—the ones telling us something is out of alignment—only leads to more frustration and deeper unhappiness. By dismissing our tension as trivial, we avoid confronting what's truly causing it, leaving us stuck in a life that isn't fulfilling, all the while convincing ourselves we should just be grateful for what we have.

The truth is, your feelings of discomfort or dissatisfaction are valid, and they're often signals that something in your life is off balance. Whether it's the way you're spending your time, managing your finances, or handling your relationships, that inner tension is your authentic self calling for attention. And while it's important to maintain perspective on the global scale of suffering, it's equally important to acknowledge the real and personal struggles that hold us back from living the lives we want.

I'd like to introduce you to three women's stories who felt trapped in different ways. While some of the names and places and details have been changed to respect their privacy each of these are real women feeling the tension between what they truly wanted for their lives and the situations they were in. Maybe you can relate to their stories.

The Problem of Regret

Paula moved to London from her home country, not speaking a word of English. She started by working in restaurants, slowly learning the language and adjusting to life in a new city. Over time, her hard work paid off—she managed to get a business degree and eventually landed a job at a top advertising agency. By the time her career took off, she had everything she'd ever dreamed of: a beautiful home in the expensive suburb of Richmond, two wonderful kids, and the luxury of designer clothes, vacations, and a comfortable lifestyle.

But as her children entered secondary school, Paula began to feel a deep sense of regret. The nanny had been the one raising her children, and Paula realized she had missed out on much of their childhood. They were growing up fast, and soon they'd be out in the world, starting lives of their own. Paula wanted to reconnect with them before it was too late, to bond with her children in a meaningful way. However, their lives required two incomes to function. When she moved to London she was pursuing a dream but now she's wondering if she had to pay too much for success and financial security.

Paula felt trapped. She was acutely aware that scaling back her hours would mean scaling back the lifestyle she and her family had grown accustomed to—mortgage, private school fees, and all the "extras" that make London life so costly. **How could she maintain the family's finances on a reduced income?** She had poured years of effort into building her career, and now it felt impossible to step away without losing the very security she'd worked so hard to achieve. Yet the price of this success was her limited connection with her children—time she could never get back. She found herself torn between the material comforts she had earned and a growing longing to be present for her family in a deeper, more meaningful way.

Paula unintentionally became trapped by her lifestyle.

The Problem of Economic Oppression

Maria and her family came to the United States from Nicaragua on an asylum visa, seeking not only safety but a chance at a life where their children could thrive. Leaving behind political turmoil and economic instability, they arrived with determination and hope. Yet from the moment they stepped off the plane, reality set in: the cost of living was immense, and each day felt like a race against mounting bills. Maria threw herself into learning English on her phone during breaks between shifts, often surviving on just a few hours of sleep.

Despite her husband also working full-time, Maria now juggles three jobs—cleaning offices before sunrise, working at a restaurant through the afternoon, and babysitting in the evenings. She dreams of being home when her children come back from school, helping with homework or simply asking about their day. Instead, she's perpetually in transit, catching buses across town to make her next shift on time. The rare moments she does spend with her kids are overshadowed by exhaustion and the worry of how they'll pay next month's rent.

Every day, she wishes she could work less but earn enough to cover basic needs. She wants to cook dinners as a family, attend school recitals, and give her children the emotional support they need— luxuries that feel painfully out of reach. Maria wonders if there's a path to true financial stability without sacrificing the precious time she yearns to share with her kids. But at this point, she can't see how to exit the cycle of relentless work that barely keeps them afloat. Despite all her determination, Maria feels trapped, living proof that hard work alone sometimes isn't enough to break free from economic oppression.

Maria's problem is time scarcity. There is just not enough time to make the money she needs to support her family and be there for her kids.

The Problem of Vulnerability

Abigail had always loved her job as a teacher. But when she and her wife had children, they made the decision together that Abigail would become a stay-at-home mom while her wife focused on her career. For a while, everything seemed perfect. They moved to an expensive suburb with top-rated schools, providing their children with the best opportunities. Abigail settled into her role at home, caring for the kids and managing the household.

However, over time, Abigail started noticing strange charges on their credit card statements—items she didn't recognize and expenses that didn't add up. When she confronted her wife, the truth came to light: her partner had been having an affair. The revelation was a devastating blow. Not only did it shake her trust and her marriage, but it also left her facing a harsh financial reality.

Abigail knew she could go back to teaching if she needed to, but they now lived in a high-cost suburb, chosen specifically for its excellent schools. On a teacher's salary, there was no way she could afford to buy or even rent a home in the same district. The stability she had counted on for her children's future was suddenly gone, and she found herself feeling trapped—forced to choose between returning to a career she loved but with limited financial means, or leaving the good schools behind.

Abigail didn't ask for this problem but sometimes life delivers us shit happens moments.

While these women come from different walks of life, they all share something in common: despite making decisions they believed would lead to happiness and security, they ended up feeling trapped and exhausted and unable to find an authentic balance between working and raising a family. Paula worked hard to achieve her career success and build the life she dreamed of, Abigail made what seemed like the right choice to stay home with her kids, and Maria did everything she could to create a better life for her family. Yet all of them found themselves stuck in a life that no longer worked for them and unable to see a clear way forward.

Maybe you can identify with their experiences—feeling like you've done everything "right," but still finding yourself trapped by the ever-growing demands of life and money. It's easy to feel stuck in this cycle, but here's the truth: **there is a way out**. In the next chapter, we'll start to change how you think about money, because the path to freedom begins with shifting your perspective. Buckle up, buttercup—it's time to rewrite the rules.

Exercise: Identifying Your Obstacles and Fears

1. **Free-Write Your Frustrations (5–10 minutes)**
   - Grab a notebook or open a blank document. Set a timer for five to ten minutes.
   - Write continuously about everything that feels challenging or impossible in your current situation. Don't hold back; just let the words flow. For example:
     - "I can't reduce my hours because I need the health insurance."
     - "I'm afraid we won't make ends meet if I switch jobs."
     - "I feel guilty about missing time with my kids, but I also need this income."

2. **Identify Root Causes or Pressures**
   - Review what you've written and circle or highlight statements that seem to carry the most weight or anxiety.
   - Ask yourself: "Is this an **external** pressure (bills, childcare costs, job market) or an **internal** belief (fear of failure, guilt, perfectionism)?"
   - Create two quick lists: **External Obstacles** and **Internal Obstacles**. Seeing which category each hurdle falls under can help you plan next steps.

By clarifying the mix of **external** and **internal** obstacles, you'll start to see where your biggest challenges lie—and how you might begin addressing them

Buckle Up, Buttercup: Changing How You Think About Money

In the previous chapter, we explored the stories of women from diverse backgrounds who all shared a common need: more time freedom and financial security to show up authentically in their lives. Even if you haven't experienced their specific issues, as working moms, we all understand this tension. We want to be there for our children, present in their lives, while also maintaining a career and financial stability. But too often, we fall into the trap of trading our time for money—working more hours, taking on more responsibilities, thinking that if we just push a little harder, everything will balance out. In reality, it doesn't. We end up exhausted, overextended, and still longing for more time and freedom.

To break free from this cycle, we need to stop thinking of the money we earn as just a means to buy a bigger lifestyle. Instead, we must change our relationship with money entirely, reframing it as a tool for creating freedom and security. This chapter sets the stage for that crucial mental shift, laying the groundwork for the practical "how-tos" that we'll dive into later. No matter where you are on your financial journey, adopting these three baseline principles are the core of the Freedom Mindset and are essential to creating the life you truly want for yourself and your family.

Principle 1: Live Below Your Means and Build a Safety Net

The first principle is simple yet powerful: **live so that your expenses never exceed your income**. For many people, living beyond their means—often through credit card debt or excessive spending—is a common trap. We upgrade our lifestyle with every raise or promotion, thinking that more income equals more room to spend. But financial freedom comes not just from avoiding debt, but from actively **underspending** and saving what's left over.

This saving isn't just for emergencies, though that's important—it's the key to breaking the time-money trap. By consistently saving, you create a financial buffer that allows you to stop relying so heavily on your paycheck. Over time, this savings will become the seed that grows into your ability to replace the need to trade your time for money.

The real challenge is to **shift your thinking**: instead of seeing money as a way to buy more things or elevate your lifestyle, start viewing it as a tool to free up your time. In Chapter Two we saw that when you fall into the habit of upgrading your lifestyle with each raise, you're only reinforcing the time-money trap. The more you spend, the more you need to keep working to maintain that lifestyle. Living below your means flips that script. Instead of your lifestyle owning you, you own it. The emotional payoff isn't deprivation—it's relief. Relief that one curveball won't topple everything. Relief that you can breathe without chasing the next raise just to cover the bills. The goal here isn't just to avoid debt—it's to actively spend less than you make so you can save, invest, and ultimately reduce the amount of time you have to trade for money in the future.

Principle 2: Make Your Money Work for You

Once you've started saving, the next principle comes into play: **make your money work so you don't have to**. The goal is to gradually replace the time you spend working for money with money that generates income for you. Over time, the money you invest should begin to provide a steady stream of income that slowly replaces the need to trade your hours for a paycheck. This transition won't happen overnight, but it is the foundation for long-term financial freedom.

Remember Maria's story? She couldn't work more hours, no matter how hard she tried. Time scarcity had already maxed her out. That's why this principle matters so much—because none of us can "outwork" the limits of time. The emotional payoff of having your money work for you isn't just more income—it's spaciousness. It's the peace of knowing that even when life pulls harder on your time, your financial foundation keeps working in the background.

The key is to shift your focus from solely earning through active work to earning through passive or leveraged income—where your investments, whether in stocks, real estate, or other vehicles, start to pay you back without requiring more of your time. As your money begins to grow and generate income, it will reduce the amount of time you need to work to maintain your lifestyle. This shift is crucial to breaking the time-money trap.

How you make your money work for you will depend on a number of factors: your personal financial goals, risk tolerance, lifestyle preferences, and current financial situation. In **Section 2** we'll dive deeper into specific strategies for investing and growing your savings. Whether you're just starting to save or already have significant assets, there are various approaches you can take to ensure that your money is being put to work in ways that align with your long-term vision for your life.

The key here is **patience and discipline**. The money you save today and invest wisely can begin to compound, providing you with returns that eventually make it possible to reduce the number of hours you need to work. Over time, you'll start to see a shift where your investments are generating enough income to replace part, or even all, of your salary. That's the real path to freedom.

Principle 3: Reframe Money as a Tool for Freedom, Not Just Spending

Finally, once you begin to shift your mindset about how you're using your money, you'll naturally start to see all your financial decisions differently. This leads us to Principle Three: **reframe money as a means of gaining more freedom and safety** rather than simply a tool for buying more things.

Abigail's story was a stark reminder of how vulnerable we can feel when our security depends on one job, one income, or one relationship. Reframing money as freedom means you build safety nets and options. The payoff here isn't a bigger house or a shinier car—it's dignity, peace, and the power to walk away from what no longer serves you. That, to me, is the true wealth. Not the number in your account, but the ability to live aligned with your values without fear holding the reins.

When you view money as a tool for freedom, every financial decision becomes more intentional. That next promotion might come with a pay raise, but is the extra income worth the time away from your family or the added stress? Or, if you're thinking about an investment opportunity, you might ask: what happens if it doesn't work out? What systems do you have in place to ensure your financial security, no matter what?

This shift in mindset helps you make decisions that prioritize **time freedom, emotional well-being, and long-term security**, rather than short-term financial gains. It allows you to create **redundancy** in your financial life—having multiple streams of income, savings, and investments that ensure you're protected, even if one thing goes wrong.

In the next section we will get into the practical how to of implementing these three principles. No matter what your starting point there is a way to make significant changes in all three areas.

Meredith and Scott: Choosing Peace Over Square Footage

Meredith and Scott were the kind of couple everyone admired. They built their life and their business together, raising three energetic boys while running a thriving local printing company. It wasn't always easy—juggling deadlines and soccer practices never is—but they loved the life they had created. It was theirs.

That all changed when Scott died suddenly. One moment he was there, cracking a joke over breakfast, and the next he was gone. The grief hit hard and fast, like a wave crashing down before Meredith even had time to steady herself.

In the aftermath, her first instinct was to cling to the familiar. Their beautiful family home was a symbol of everything they had worked for—a place where memories were etched into every room, from the height marks on the kitchen wall to the creak in the floorboards that Scott used to joke about fixing. Letting go of the house felt unthinkable.

But the reality of their finances made her think again. The mortgage, once manageable with two incomes, loomed like a dark cloud over her head. Every month, the stress of making the payment chipped away at her. She felt it in her chest, in her sleep, and in the shortness of her temper.

One night, sitting at the kitchen table with bills spread out in front of her, Meredith looked at her boys—ages 10, 8, and 5—and realized they deserved better. They didn't need the house. They needed *her*. Not the stressed, snappy, constantly-worrying-about-money version of her, but the mom who laughed with them over dinner and showed up to their games without a phone glued to her hand.

The decision wasn't easy, but it was clear. Meredith sold the house and downsized to a smaller one that kept the boys in their same school district. It wasn't what she had pictured for their future, but as she settled into the new place, she realized it was what they needed.

Without the crushing weight of the mortgage, Meredith could breathe again. She continued her work at the printing business she and Scott had built, finding comfort in keeping a piece of his legacy alive while being present for her kids. The house wasn't as big, and the yard wasn't as grand, but her boys didn't seem to mind.

In fact, they thrived. And so did she. Meredith discovered that the key to moving forward wasn't clinging to what had been, but finding a way to create peace in what was.

"My boys needed me more than they needed a big house," she reflects now. "And honestly? I needed me too."

Exercise: Where Do Your Ideas About Money Need an Upgrade?

To help you identify where you might need to rethink your relationship with money, consider the following questions and journal on them:

- **Are you living beyond your means?** Take an honest look at your spending habits. Are there areas where you're overspending or relying on debt?
- **How much of your money is working for you?** How much of your savings or investments are generating income? Are there opportunities to invest more and start creating passive income streams?
- **What contingencies do you have in place?** If something unexpected happened—such as a job loss or family

emergency—how prepared would you be financially? Do you have a solid financial safety net in place?

This exercise is designed to help you reflect on your current money mindset and identify areas where you can start to make changes. Remember, the goal isn't just to make more money—it's to create more **freedom** and **security** for yourself and your family.

Section II: The Freedom Mindset Shift

In the previous section, we explored why simply having "a seat at the table" isn't enough for women who crave both time freedom and financial stability. Traditional workplace structures often leave us overworked, under-recognized, or bound by rigid rules that don't accommodate the realities of modern life—particularly motherhood. Now it's time to shift our perspective and build a pathway that grants genuine independence and choice.

This section walks you through the fundamentals of building a Freedom Mindset. We'll start by laying down the fundamentals of making money (and why a paycheck alone might not cut it), then dive into calculating your baseline—the amount you need to stand on your own two feet financially, or what I affectionately call "fuck-you money." Finally, we'll bring it all together by examining how income, expenses, and investments can flow in a way that supports your ultimate goals of freedom and security. Consider these chapters your roadmap for reclaiming both your time and your earning power.

CHAPTER 4

We All Need Fuck-You Money: Calculating Your Freedom Baseline

If money weren't a factor in your decisions, what would change?

Would you finally have the option to work less and be more present for your kids? Would you leave a job that drains you? Would you take time off to write that book, start a passion project, or travel? Would you stop tolerating a relationship, a boss, or a situation that no longer serves you?

For most of us, financial stress isn't just about not having enough—it's about not knowing if we'll keep having enough. The constant "what if?" plays in the background: *What if I lose my job? What if my partner's income disappears? What if something unexpected happens, and I can't afford to recover?*

We're taught that financial security means making more money. But that's only part of the equation. True financial security isn't just about earning a good paycheck—because as long as your paycheck is the only thing keeping your life stable, you're still vulnerable.

The real goal isn't just income. It's income that keeps flowing even if you stop working.

That's where the concept of your **Freedom Baseline** comes in. Your Freedom Baseline is the cost of your basic living expenses, the minimum amount you need each month to keep your life stable. The goal is to build up enough passive or low-maintenance income streams that don't require you to trade time for a paycheck to cover this Freedom Baseline. When you reach that point, you're no longer forced to work just to survive. You have options.

And this is what freedom really means. It's not about luxury vacations or sprawling homes. It's about not being forced to do things you don't want to because of money. It's about having the security to say *no* to situations that don't align with your values or your well-being. It's about being able to negotiate with confidence, take time off when your family needs you, or walk away from what no longer serves you.

Imagine the power of being able to walk into your boss's office and negotiate a raise or a flexible schedule, knowing that if the answer is "no," you'll still be okay. Imagine the peace of mind that comes from knowing that if you need to step away from work to care for an aging loved one, you can. This level of financial security is priceless, and it gives you a freedom that's often reserved for the wealthy. But it's not about being rich—it's about being free from financial fear.

For me, this is the definition of **true wealth**—not how much you make—but how much peace, choice, and time you own.

What Is Freedom, Really?

Think about it: how many of us have stayed in jobs we didn't love, put up with treatment we didn't deserve, or let go of dreams we cherished—all because we needed the paycheck? At some point, we've all had to make compromises in the name of financial survival. This feeling is so common that it's sometimes called the prostitute archetype—selling parts of ourselves, our time, and even our dreams for money. And while it may feel necessary, it doesn't have to be permanent.

While the Instagram-worthy "rich life" might sound great, what we're talking about here is far more valuable. Real wealth isn't just numbers in a bank account; **it's the ability to decide how you spend your days**, to step back when your family needs you, to work in a way that aligns with your values rather than just your bills. It's about being able to design a life that works for you, rather than squeezing yourself into a system that wasn't built for working moms.

Once your Freedom Baseline is covered—whether through investments, rental income, a small business that runs without you, or other assets—you have something most people never get: real choice. You can take a break without financial panic. You can take risks, invest in yourself, and make decisions that align with your values instead of your bank balance. You gain leverage—the ability to negotiate from a place of power rather than desperation.

And most importantly? You gain control over your time. Because at the end of the day, time is the one resource you can never earn back.

And when your income is no longer tied to every hour you work, you gain the flexibility to be the kind of mom, partner, friend, and woman you truly want to be.

In this chapter, we'll go step by step through how to calculate your Freedom Baseline, how to shrink it without feeling deprived, and why hitting this number should be your first financial goal. Because freedom starts when your survival doesn't depend on a paycheck—and once you have that foundation, everything else becomes easier.

When you have your Freedom Baseline covered by passive income, you're no longer at the mercy of any one job or employer. You can make choices that align with who you are, rather than who you need to be to pay the bills. And that's what real freedom is about. It's not about living extravagantly; it's about knowing you have the security to make decisions that honor your life and values.

But before you can reach that point, you need to know your number.

Calculating Your Freedom Baseline

Now let's talk about how you can calculate your own Freedom Baseline. This isn't a magic number that requires perfection or extensive financial knowledge. It's a simple calculation of the essentials—just enough to keep things stable, cover your needs, and ensure your security.

Here's how to do it:

1. **Housing** – Rent or mortgage, property taxes, and basic maintenance. Just the cost of keeping a roof over your head.
2. **Utilities** – Electricity, water, gas, internet, phone—keeping the basics running.
3. **Food** – Groceries and essentials. Not dining out, just what keeps everyone fed.
4. **Transportation** – Car payments, insurance, gas, or public transit. Reliable ways to get where you need to go.
5. **Insurance** – Health insurance premiums and other essential coverage.
6. **Healthcare** – Regular expenses like medications or routine appointments.
7. **Debt Payments** – Only necessary payments on "essential" debts, like a car loan or student loan.

Add these amounts together, and you'll have your Freedom Baseline—the bare minimum you need each month to stay safe and secure. This is the number you'll aim to cover with passive income, so that, in time, you have the freedom to make choices without financial fear.

Ways to Reduce Your Freedom Baseline

The lower your Freedom Baseline, the easier it is to cover it with passive income. Reducing expenses isn't about deprivation—it's about being intentional so you can create freedom faster. And if reducing your baseline doesn't resonate for you, that's okay too—it may just take longer to build the income streams to cover it.

Some strategies to consider:

- **Downsize if possible.** Housing is usually the biggest expense. Moving to a smaller place, a more affordable area, or renting out a room can accelerate your path.
- **Cut back on non-essentials.** Redirecting even small amounts from dining out, premium subscriptions, or impulse buys can make freedom attainable sooner.
- **Optimize your bills.** Negotiate utilities, bundle insurance, meal-plan groceries, or switch to lower-cost cell providers. Small shifts add up.
- **Buy used.** Furniture, electronics, kids' gear—secondhand can save thousands while keeping good items out of landfills.
- **Rethink car ownership.** Reliable used cars, fewer cars per household, or even biking and transit for short commutes. Cars are one of the fastest ways to sabotage financial freedom.
- **Embrace the sharing economy.** Borrow, rent, or swap instead of buying outright.
- **DIY within reason.** Cooking, basic maintenance, brewing your own coffee. Small things, big impact.
- **Travel smarter.** Off-season trips, points, or home exchanges reduce costs without losing the joy.
- **Get creative with housing costs.** Refinancing, negotiating rent, or house-hacking with roommates can all lower your baseline.

Lowering your baseline isn't about restriction—it's about trading unnecessary expenses for security and choice. Every dollar saved shrinks the amount of income you need, making freedom attainable without being trapped by a paycheck.

Freedom Isn't Just Financial—It's Emotional

Reaching your Freedom Baseline isn't just about making the numbers work—it's about what those numbers represent. It's about the shift from survival mode to intentional living.

When your essential needs are covered without trading every hour for a paycheck, something profound happens: your brain stops operating from fear. You stop making choices out of financial anxiety, and you start making them based on what truly matters— to you, to your family, to your future.

Imagine the peace that comes with knowing that no job, no boss, no unexpected life event can completely upend your world. Imagine what it feels like to **work because you want to, not because you have to.**

This is what we call fuck-you money—the ability to walk away from anything that doesn't serve you. It's not about rebellion for the sake of it, or accumulating wealth just to have it. **It's about power—the power to choose.**

Because real financial freedom isn't about having more. It's about needing less—and knowing that your life, your choices, and your time belong to you.

Sheila's Story: Building Freedom on Her Own Terms

Let's look at an example: Sheila's story. Sheila worked in the corporate world for years, and she was actually happy there. She liked her job, the challenge, and the sense of purpose it gave her. But Sheila was also a planner, and she wanted to ensure she'd have options down the road. Even though she enjoyed her job, she didn't want to be forced to stay if circumstances changed or if she wanted to explore something new. So, she made a plan.

While working full-time, Sheila began to build her own freedom. Instead of spending her entire paycheck, she saved aggressively and bought her first rental property. At first, it was just one small property, a modest duplex that provided a little extra income. She handled the property management herself, collecting rent, managing repairs, and getting familiar with the process. It wasn't glamorous, but Sheila saw it as a stepping stone.

Over the years, Sheila used the rental income and her savings to buy more properties. By her forties, she had accumulated enough passive income from these properties to cover her basic expenses—her Freedom Baseline. This gave her a profound sense of security. When her corporate job started requiring more travel and longer hours, she decided it was time to leave. Thanks to her rental income, she could afford to make that choice.

But Sheila didn't stop there. Free from her corporate obligations, she had time to explore her creative side. She took on consulting work on her own terms, picking projects that excited her and left plenty of time for her passion for painting. With her Freedom

Baseline covered, Sheila was able to create a life that reflected her true self, rather than one dictated by financial necessity.

Sheila's story isn't about becoming rich in a conventional sense; it's about creating a life with choices. By building passive income streams that covered her Freedom Baseline, she transformed her life from one where she had to work to one where she got to work. And that's the power of knowing your Freedom Baseline.

When you boil it down, each of these principles is less about money and more about liberation. Lifestyle creep, time scarcity, and life's curveballs will always be waiting in the wings—but adopting this mindset keeps them from owning you. The true wealth isn't just financial. It's the calm of knowing you're safe, the joy of having time for what matters most, and the strength of being able to choose your own path.

Exercise: Calculate Your Freedom Baseline

Take some time to calculate your own Freedom Baseline. Grab a pen and paper, or open up a spreadsheet, and go through each essential category. List out your monthly housing costs, utilities, food expenses, transportation, insurance, healthcare, and necessary debt payments. Add them up, and you'll have your personal Freedom Baseline.

This number represents the first step on your journey to financial freedom. It's the amount you want to cover with passive income, so that no matter what happens, you have security. And even if you're not there yet, knowing this number gives you a goal—a reminder of what you're working toward.

Conclusion: The Foundation of Financial Freedom

Your Freedom Baseline isn't just a financial calculation—it's the foundation for a life where you own your choices instead of being owned by your circumstances. When your baseline is covered, you don't have to stay in a job you hate, tolerate situations that don't serve you, or sacrifice what matters most just to make ends meet. Instead, you gain something far more valuable than money: options.

But understanding your baseline is only step one. The next step is figuring out how to fund it—without being stuck in the endless loop of trading time for money. Because while financial security starts with knowing what you need, true financial freedom happens when your income is no longer completely dependent on your labor.

So, now that you know how much you need to reach your Freedom Baseline, the million-dollar question is: How do you actually make that money?

The answer starts with understanding the different ways income is earned, the trade-offs of each, and how you can start shifting your income streams to create more freedom and security in your life.

Let's dive into that next.

CHAPTER 5

How to Make Money 101

Shifting from Making a Living to Building a Life

In the last chapter, you calculated your Freedom Baseline—the minimum amount you need to feel secure. Knowing your number is powerful, but here's the next question: where does that money actually come from?

Most of us grow up with the same fundamental belief about money: you work, you get paid. End of story. We internalize this early—whether from watching our parents punch the clock, getting our first hourly wage job, or being told that "good jobs" are the key to security. Trading time for money feels like the only option because it's the only one we're taught.

But what if that's only the starting point?

If you've ever felt like you're working harder but not getting ahead, constantly balancing job stress and family life, or wishing there was more flexibility in how you earn—you're not alone. The traditional income model wasn't built with women (or mothers) in mind. And if your entire Freedom Baseline depends on that one model, you'll always feel vulnerable.

This chapter is about expanding your view of how money can flow into your life. While most of us inevitably start by trading time for money, that doesn't mean it's the only path. By understanding the different ways people create income, you can start making choices that both fund your baseline and align with your values.

The Three Ways to Make Money

Even though it appears like there are infinite ways to make money and so many things that people do professionally, at the most basic level, there are only three ways to generate income:

1. **Trading Time for Money**
2. **Creating or Buying an Asset That Earns Money**
3. **Building a System (aka a Business) That Generates Income**

No method is inherently good or bad. Each has its own risks and rewards, and each may fit you differently at different ages or stages of life. Most financially free people eventually use a combination of all three. That's part of the payoff: the more diverse your streams of income, the steadier your foundation becomes. If one quadrant gets wobbly—say, your job disappears or an investment underperforms—the others keep your baseline covered. That redundancy is where real peace of mind comes from.

So why do so many women stay stuck in the first quadrant—trading time for money? It's not just because jobs feel predictable or safe. It's also because of what we're taught (and not taught) about money.

Think about it: how many girls grow up with parents, mentors, or friends who ask, "What kind of business would you like to own someday?" How many are encouraged to save their babysitting money and open an investment account instead of spending it at the mall? Did your mom ever sit you down at the kitchen table to look at real estate listings and explain how buying a property could build long-term wealth? Mine didn't. Most don't.

Instead, girls are often nudged toward stability and security: "Get a good job, don't take too many risks, make sure you have benefits." Meanwhile, boys are more likely to hear messages about investing, ownership, or entrepreneurship. The result is that many women don't even realize there are options beyond trading time for money until later in life—sometimes when the pressures of caregiving, burnout, or a financial crisis force them to start looking.

That's why understanding the other methods matters so much. It's not about quitting your job tomorrow. It's about expanding your awareness so you're not boxed into the narrow path you were handed. Because freedom comes when you have more than one way to fund your baseline.

And here's the best part: it's not too late to start. Even if no one showed you these options early on, you can learn them now—and once you do, the way you think about earning will never be the same. From tech CEOs to small-town entrepreneurs to moms building side hustles during nap time, every path to income boils down to just three models. When you understand these three, you have a framework to evaluate where you are today, where you want to go, and how to create the kind of freedom a paycheck alone can't buy.

Let's take them one by one.

Trading Time for Money

This is where most of us start: we trade our time for a paycheck. In this approach, you're compensated based on the hours or tasks you complete. Trading time for money is the most common way people earn a living because it's accessible, predictable, and provides a sense of security.

In this category, there are generally two main paths:

- **Employee:** You work for someone else in exchange for a paycheck. For many moms, a steady job offers structure, stability, and often benefits like healthcare or retirement plans. It's a way to contribute to your family's income while having some predictable hours and responsibilities.
- **Solopreneur:** You work for yourself—freelancing, consulting, or running a one-person business. While you're not working for an employer, you still need to "show up" and work to earn. Solopreneurship offers more flexibility, but your income still depends on your active participation. When you don't work, you don't get paid.

Trading time for money has its perks. It offers predictable income, making it easier to plan and budget for your family's needs. For employees, it's also a chance to learn new skills, build professional networks, and gain experience—all on "other people's money."

Unless you inherited wealth or started investing young, this is where most of us *have* to begin. You need income before you can grow income. A paycheck isn't the endgame, but it's the launchpad for saving, investing, and eventually creating assets or businesses.

The downside is clear. When your income is tied directly to your working hours, it limits your earning potential. There are only so many hours in a day. If you stop working, the income stops. And solopreneurs face the extra burden of wearing all the hats—client work, bookkeeping, marketing, admin—often while balancing family life.

Still, this stage can be a powerful foundation. Think of it as your training ground—the place where you develop the discipline, habits, and seed money that will fuel your next stage of growth.

Creating or Buying an Asset That Makes Money While You Sleep

Even if you love your work, there's something powerful about waking up to find that money came in overnight. It means your security isn't tied only to the hours you put in that day. This second method of making money involves building or buying assets that generate income with far less daily involvement from you.

This is the start of creating what's often called *passive income*. But let's be clear: no income stream is ever completely passive. Every asset requires some upfront work or ongoing oversight. A better term might be *lower-maintenance income*—because once the foundation is in place, the income keeps flowing without constant effort.

Examples of lower-maintenance, income-generating assets include:

- **Investment Accounts:** Stocks, bonds, mutual funds, or even high-interest savings accounts that grow in value through market gains and dividends.
- **E-Course:** Create it once, and sell it repeatedly. Each new student generates income without you reinventing the wheel.
- **Rental Property:** Real estate can provide reliable monthly income, though it requires initial effort and occasional management.

The benefits are profound. Lower-maintenance income streams give you freedom to step away from constant hustling and create space for family, creativity, or simply breathing room. Over time, these assets compound, moving you closer to a future where your money works for you.

The trade-off: building assets requires resources—either upfront money (to buy them) or upfront time (to create them). They also come with risks: market fluctuations, vacancies, or the need for ongoing maintenance. But even with these challenges, they're a critical stepping stone between "earning only when you work" and true financial freedom.

Creating a System (aka a Business) That Generates Income

The third approach to making money is to create a system—a.k.a. a business that generates income even when you're not directly involved. At its core, that's what a business really is: a system that, once built, allows money to flow whether or not you show up every day.

This distinction is critical. Many people think they own a business when, in reality, they've just created another job. The difference between a solopreneur and a true business owner is this: if you take a week off, does the money keep coming in? If the answer is no, you're still trading time for money.

Take a home-based bakery as an example. If you're doing all the baking, packaging, and selling yourself, the money stops when you stop. But if you invest in a team, document your recipes, and streamline your processes, the bakery can run without you. That's when you've crossed the line into ownership.

The magic of this shift is scalability. A well-built business can grow beyond your own hours or energy. It can eventually run with minimal involvement from you, giving you time freedom and creating a true asset that can be sold, passed down, or maintained for years.

Of course, this doesn't happen overnight. Building systems and teams requires skill and patience. But the reward is immense: once your business can operate without you, you've achieved a level of freedom that's hard to reach through jobs or investments alone.

Financial Evolution: Moving Through the Quadrants

Think of these three approaches—trading time for money, creating assets, and building a business—as a roadmap for your financial evolution. Each stage represents a different level of freedom and requires different skills and mindset shifts.

Not every asset or business idea succeeds, and not every job is secure. But even failed attempts build resilience, knowledge, and opportunities for the next step. The point isn't perfection— it's progression. Step by step, you move from earning a living to building a life.

And with each shift—from trading time, to owning assets, to building systems—you're not just adding dollars. You're adding choice, breathing room, and leverage. That's the true wealth: freedom on your own terms.

A Blueprint for Financial Growth

EMPLOYEE

- Income comes from another person's business
- Great opportunity to learn skills and take risks with "other people's money"
- Focus will be on personally managing your saving, spending and investing to provide a stable
- base and using your money to express your values and passions

BUSINESS OWNER

- May start, grow or buy a business which now has employees to manage and pay but who also create structure around income generation
- Beginning of the ability to "make money while you sleep"
- Challenges become management; delegation and how to strategically grow especially when faced with conflicting priorities or multiple opportunities
- Team dynamics and conflicting money styles can be working subconsciously

SOLOPRENEUR

- Often takes the skills and talents developed as an employee to now work for yourself
- Income comes from your ability to "show up and make it happen"
- Often need to learn skills that were previously done by "someone else" such as bookkeeping or marketing
- Challenges are building additional passive income channels as well as mastering the personal finance skills of the previous quadrant

INVESTOR

- Qualified investors can become equity partners in other people's businesses – this may or may not involve holding a Board position or acting in an advisory role
- The challenge is understanding the risks and rewards of owning part of another business with minimal control over day to day operations
- Can be a fabulous way to build significant passive income and to assist other entrepreneurs move to the next quadrant

The chart on Page 61 summarizes the four ways of making money: trading time for income, either as an employee or a solopreneur, creating lower maintenance income assets and building self-sustaining businesses. Each comes with its own benefits and trade-offs, but together they create a framework for freedom.

Remember: every dollar you save or invest is a step away from being trapped by your hours and closer to a life with options. In the next chapters, we'll dig into how to manage what you earn across your core categories—living costs, lifestyle, and savings—so you can maximize every resource in service of freedom.

Because ultimately, the power of money isn't in how much you have. **It's in the choices it gives you, the security it creates, and the time it frees to live the life you want.**

Story of Caitlyn's Journey Through the Quadrants

Caitlyn always dreamed of becoming a hairdresser. After graduating from beauty school, she was thrilled to land a position at an elite salon in Chicago—a prestigious hire that felt like the pinnacle of her early career. At first, everything seemed perfect. She loved the high-end environment, the steady stream of clients, and the glamour of working in a well-known establishment.

But the shine wore off quickly. Caitlyn realized that making good money was harder than she had anticipated. The salon took a substantial cut of her earnings, charging her not only for a portion of each service but also for supplies and laundry. Even worse, she had little control over her time. She was required to be at the salon during set hours, even if she didn't have bookings. It wasn't just the money that began to chafe—it was the lack of freedom.

This setup became unbearable after Caitlyn had her first child. The long hours at the salon, combined with the costs of childcare, made her financial situation feel increasingly unsustainable. She hated being away from her baby, especially during hours when she wasn't even earning. Something had to change.

With the support of family and friends, Caitlyn decided to strike out on her own. She rented a small salon space, becoming a solopreneur. The overhead of rent was intimidating at first, but she quickly realized that she was taking home more money than she had as an employee. The freedom to set her own hours also meant she could prioritize time with her daughter without sacrificing income.

It wasn't long before Caitlyn saw another opportunity: collaboration. She rented out the extra chairs in her salon to other independent hairdressers, women who, like her, wanted to work for themselves. The chair rentals not only covered the cost of the salon's rent but also provided Caitlyn with additional income. She was building a business model that didn't rely solely on her own labor.

As Caitlyn's income grew, she continued to save. Instead of spending the extra money, she used it to buy a small apartment, which she rented out for additional income. This rental income gave her another layer of financial security. Over time, she saved enough to buy a larger salon space—this time in a building she owned. Now, the rent from the chairs wasn't going to someone else's mortgage; it was building her own wealth.

Best of all, Caitlyn had the flexibility she had always wanted. If she didn't have a client booked, she could take the afternoon off to spend time with her daughter. Her business was no longer dependent entirely on her presence.

Her success didn't stop there. When one of the women renting a chair from Caitlyn decided to open her own salon, Caitlyn saw an opportunity to pay it forward. She came in as an investor, taking a percentage of the profits without needing to work in the new salon herself. In doing so, she helped another woman take her first steps toward financial independence, just as Caitlyn's own family and friends had helped her.

Caitlyn's story is one of transformation—not just for her own life but for others around her. She moved from being an employee with no control over her time and income to becoming an entrepreneur, investor, and mentor. Her journey is a testament to the power of stepping into new roles, taking calculated risks, and creating opportunities for others along the way.

Exercise: Mapping Your Income Streams

1. **List Your Current Income Sources**
   - Write down every way you earn money right now—salary, freelance work, side gigs, rental income, dividends, etc.
   - Decide which **quadrant** each income source belongs to:
     - **Employee** (someone else's payroll)
     - **Solopreneur** (your own business, but you're the main doer)

- - **Business Owner** (you employ others or have a system that earns money independently of your direct labor)
  - **Investor** (your money is working in someone else's venture, real estate, or paper assets)

2. **Reflect on Your Income Balance**
   - Observe how much of your overall earnings come from each quadrant. Does one quadrant dominate? Are you relying on only one or two sources?
   - Ask yourself what you **like** about your current setup and what **concerns** you. For instance, are you overly dependent on a single paycheck, or do you crave more diversity in your streams of income?

3. **Brainstorm New Quadrant Opportunities**
   - Identify **one** quadrant you'd like to explore more. Maybe you're an Employee who wants to try Solopreneurship, or a Solopreneur who'd like to invest in another person's venture.
   - Sketch out a few possible ways to generate income in that new quadrant. For example:
     - **If Employee to Solopreneur**: Could you turn a current hobby into a paid service?
     - **If Solopreneur to Business Owner**: Can you hire help or build systems to reduce your hands-on hours?
     - **If Business Owner to Investor**: Could you buy into someone else's startup or real estate deal?

○   Write down any questions or concerns that come to mind. These "unknowns" are often the best place to focus your learning and planning.

Next Steps:

By clarifying where you stand now and where you want to go, you can start seeking out resources, mentors, or opportunities in that new quadrant. This might mean taking a course, lining up financing, or simply talking to someone who's already there. Above all, remember that moving from one quadrant to another is a process—it may feel daunting, but each step you take brings you closer to a more balanced and intentional income portfolio.

CHAPTER 6

Savings Is Not a Four-Letter Word

The whole idea of making your money work for you so you don't have to work forever is based on one unavoidable fact: **you have to have money to put to work in the first place.**

If, like me, you weren't born with a trust fund, then the only way to build up that money is to **learn how to save.**

Why Saving Matters

Saving is the first skill that makes everything else possible—it's what gives you the seed capital to start investing, buy a business, or create financial freedom. Yet for many people, the word *saving* triggers the same feeling as another dreaded four-letter word: *diet*.

No one likes cutting back—whether it's calories or expenses. But saving doesn't have to feel like deprivation. Just like dieting isn't about starving yourself—it's about fueling your body wisely— saving isn't about denying yourself everything. It's about creating **options, freedom, and security.**

If you're barely making ends meet, hearing "just save more" can feel infuriating. But the truth is this: the only way to make your money work for you is to have money to work with. That doesn't mean you need to live a miserly, joyless existence. With the right mindset and a few creative strategies, saving can actually feel empowering—even fun.

Shift Your Mindset

Instead of seeing saving as giving something up, reframe it as **buying your own freedom.** Every dollar you put away isn't about denying yourself a small pleasure today—it's about purchasing the life you want tomorrow.

Ten Ways to Make Saving Easier

1. Don't Have a Budget—Have a Daily Spending Cap

I **hate budgets**. They're complicated, hard to stick to, and often don't reflect real life. Traditional budgeting involves tracking categories, analyzing where your money goes, and constantly updating spreadsheets. Who has time for that?

Instead, calculate a **daily spending cap**:

- Start with your monthly income.
- Subtract fixed expenses (rent, insurance, utilities, car payments, minimum debt payments).
- Whatever's left is your discretionary spending.
- Divide that number by 30.

If you have $900 left after essentials, that's $30 per day.

Now, is this system perfect? No. But it gives you a clear, easy-to-track metric—if you go over your cap one day, you can balance it out by spending less another day. It keeps spending in check without the rigidity of a traditional budget.

2. When You Deprive Yourself, Save the Difference

A lot of people say no to small expenses—they skip the daily latte, pack their lunch, or walk instead of taking an Uber. That's great! The problem is, most never **actually save** that money.

It's not enough to just *not spend*—you need to **intentionally move** that money into savings.

Here's the rule: Every time you forgo an expense, transfer that amount into savings. Don't put it in a jar—use a high-yield savings account so it grows while you keep building the habit.

- Skipped a $6 coffee? Transfer $6.
- Packed lunch instead of spending $15? Transfer $15.
- Free activity instead of a $50 concert? Transfer $50.

At first, it might feel small, but this habit **adds up fast**. Instead of just feeling virtuous about skipping something, you'll *see* a tangible financial reward.

3. Play the No-Spend Day Challenge

I love playing a game: **How many days can I go without spending money?**

Having *No-Spend Days* forces you to be more resourceful, rethink impulse purchases, and use what you already have. It's amazing how much we spend on autopilot—this exercise brings awareness to what's *truly* necessary.

Try:

- Cooking with what's already in your fridge.
- Using the library instead of buying an e-book.
- Finding free entertainment—hikes, game nights, or community events.

Then, at the end of a no-spend day, transfer your daily spending cap into savings.

4. Pick Your "One Rich Thing"

Trying to "lifestyle" every aspect of your life is the quickest way to go broke. The truth is, most people can't afford to have a luxury wardrobe, a high-end car, lavish vacations, and a beautifully decorated home. But you *can* afford to pick **one** thing that makes you feel rich.

For me, that's travel. I don't care about clothes—I wear whatever is comfortable. My daughter jokes that I sometimes look borderline homeless (not really, but you get the idea). I also don't care about cars—mine is purely functional. I actually drive a 30-year-old car I bought for $2,000.

But travel? That's what makes life feel rich for me. That's where I put my extra money, guilt-free. So, ask yourself: **What's your "one rich thing"?**

Maybe it's eating at great restaurants. Maybe it's beauty treatments or wellness experiences. Maybe it's a hobby like skiing or scuba diving.

Whatever it is, prioritize it. Just make sure you're cutting back on the things that don't truly matter to you—that's where the savings come from.

5. Automate It Like a Tax

People pay their taxes automatically. You don't "accidentally" forget to pay your income tax because it's taken out of your paycheck before you even see it. So why not do the same for your savings?

- Set up **automatic transfers** so a percentage of every paycheck goes directly into your high-interest savings account before you even have a chance to spend it.
- Treat it as **non-negotiable**—like a bill you owe to your future self.

Pro Tip: If your employer allows it, split your direct deposit so a portion of your paycheck goes straight into a separate savings account. You'll be amazed at how much you can accumulate when you don't even see the money sitting in your checking account, waiting to be spent.

6. Use the 24-Hour Rule for Impulse Purchases

How often have you bought something in the moment—only to later realize you didn't actually need it?

For any non-essential purchase over say $50 or $100, wait 24 hours before buying.

- Still want it tomorrow? Fine.
- Usually, the impulse fades—and you've just "saved" that money instead.

Pro move: transfer the unspent money into savings.

7. Turn Wants into Savings Goals

Most people fail at saving because it feels like a vague, endless task—like some chore you're supposed to do forever with no real reward. The trick? **Tie your savings to something meaningful.**

- Instead of thinking *"I should save more money,"* make it specific:
    - "I want a $5,000 'freedom fund' so I can take a sabbatical or quit my job if needed."
    - "I want to save $10,000 to buy my first rental property."
    - "I want to save $3,000 for a dream trip to Thailand."

Now, every time you put money aside, it's not a *loss*—it's a step toward something exciting.

8. Try Round-Up Apps and "Invisible" Transfers

Make saving painless:

- Round-up apps take every purchase (e.g., $3.75 → $4.00) and stash the change.
- Apps like Digit or Qapital quietly transfer small amounts into savings behind the scenes.

You won't notice—but your account will.

9. Get a Money Buddy

If you've ever had more success sticking to a workout routine because you had a friend to keep you accountable, the same strategy can work for savings.

Find a **"Money Buddy"**—a friend, partner, or family member who also wants to improve their savings habits—and do it *together*.

- Check in weekly or monthly on your savings goals.
- Set a shared challenge—like who can have the most "No Spend Days" in a month **or** who can put the most in their savings account by the end of the quarter.
- Celebrate wins together (without spending money, of course!).

Having someone else in the game with you makes it easier to stay motivated—and *actually* stick to it.

10. The Salary Raise Trick

Most people increase spending when they get a raise or bonus. Instead, save half.

If your income jumps by $500/month, save $250 and spend $250.

Get a quarterly or year-end bonus? Congratulations! Use half to treat yourself but save the rest.

You'll feel the boost, but your savings will grow just as fast.

Where to Focus at Each Stage

Pre-Kids, Not Married *(Congrats! You're already thinking ahead—this is the best time to secure your financial freedom.)*

- Live with roommates or family as long as possible.
- Avoid credit card debt.
- Max out your 401(k) match—it's free money.
- Build a 3–6 month emergency fund.

Married, No Kids *(You have dual incomes—use them wisely!)*

- Budget life on one income, save the other.
- Start investing in income-producing assets.
- Guard against lifestyle creep.

Married with Kids *(Here's where smart financial choices become even more critical.)*

- Run the numbers: sometimes renting makes more sense than buying.
- Prioritize flexibility—income streams that adapt to family demands.
- Weigh childcare costs carefully against a second income.

Final Thought: Saving = Options

Saving money isn't about deprivation—it's about buying choices.

Every dollar you save today is a future "yes": yes to quitting a job you hate, yes to starting a business, yes to taking a break when you need one.

The goal isn't to hoard money. It's to build the freedom to live on your own terms.

And when you start saving with that perspective, you'll see that **it's not a burden—it's an investment in your own freedom.**

CHAPTER 7

Bringing It All Together—How Money Flows in Your Life

Throughout this book, we've explored how to break free from trading time for money, build a solid financial foundation, and set yourself up for freedom. Now, it's time to look at the bigger picture.

Financial security isn't just about **how much** money you make—it's about **how money moves** in your life. Your ability to achieve freedom depends on the flow of income and expenses, and whether you are directing enough toward **assets** that generate passive income.

This chapter maps out those flows using the **Freedom Finance Model** (aka, your Money Machine Roadmap). You'll see how money moves through your life and where you can start making shifts today.

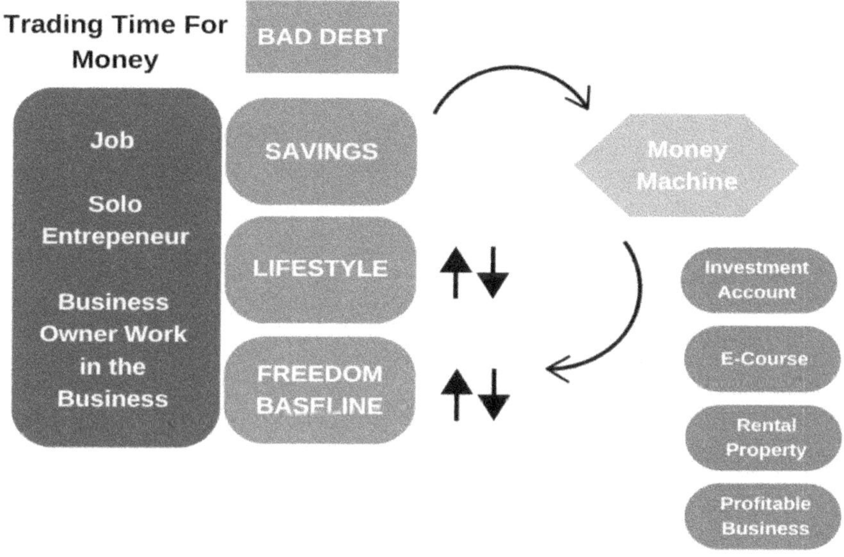

The Financial Flow Model: Understanding Where Money Goes

At this point, we've already explored the three primary ways to make money—**trading time for money, buying or creating assets, and building a self-sustaining business.** These are the three ways money flows into your life. Now let's examine what happens after you earn money and how those choices impact your financial trajectory.

When income enters your life, it can flow in **three possible directions:**

1. Freedom Baseline (Essential Expenses)

This covers the non-negotiables: housing, food, healthcare, utilities, and transportation—everything you need to survive.

- ⬆ **This number increases** when you take on a bigger mortgage, move to a higher-cost area, or increase fixed expenses.
- ⬇ **It decreases** when you downsize, eliminate unnecessary costs, or optimize expenses.

2. Lifestyle (Discretionary Spending)

These are the things that make life enjoyable—vacations, entertainment, subscriptions, dining out, hobbies.

- ⬆ **This increases** when you upgrade your lifestyle without increasing income or assets to support it.
- ⬇ **It decreases** when you choose to prioritize savings over unnecessary spending.

3. Savings (The Key to Your Money Machine)

This is **the most important category** because it determines your ability to shift from working for money to having money work for you. Savings is the **fuel** for the Money Machine.

- ⬆ **This increases** when you control lifestyle spending and allocate more income toward assets.
- ⬇ **It decreases** when expenses and bad debt eat away at your income.

The key to financial freedom is to increase your savings rate so that more money flows into assets—your Money Machine—rather than being consumed by expenses.

However, there's one major factor that blocks this flow: debt.

Debt: The Freedom Killer

There's a fourth factor that is critical to address: **bad debt.**

If your expenses consistently exceed your income, you're financing your lifestyle with debt. This might look like carrying balances on credit cards, taking out loans to cover everyday expenses, or living paycheck to paycheck with no buffer.

Bad debt is like a Reverse Money Machine. Instead of compounding your savings into income-producing assets, it compounds your spending into ever-growing interest payments. A Money Machine buys you freedom over time. A Reverse Money Machine traps you by stealing tomorrow's income to pay for yesterday's choices.

This isn't about shame or judgment. Many people fall into this cycle because of circumstances beyond their control—medical bills, job loss, or simply the cost of surviving in an expensive world. The key is recognizing the pattern and stopping the flow in the wrong direction. Even small steps—cutting unnecessary expenses, finding ways to earn more, or negotiating lower rates—help shift the machine back in your favor.

How Debt Reverses the Flow

- **It steals from your savings.** Instead of directing money into assets, you're paying for past purchases with interest.
- **It raises your Freedom Baseline.** Monthly debt payments become fixed costs, which means you need more income just to cover survival.
- **It reduces flexibility.** High debt keeps you locked in—unable to cut back work hours, take risks, or pursue opportunities that could create long-term wealth.

Debt often *masquerades* as freedom because it lets you buy things now, but in reality, it keeps you working longer just to pay for the past.

How to Flip the Machine

To shift toward financial freedom, the first step is to **shut down the Reverse Money Machine** by eliminating high-interest consumer debt:

- Pay off credit cards aggressively.
- Avoid car loans that lock you into never-ending payments.
- Refinance or consolidate high-interest loans when possible.

Every dollar you redirect away from debt repayment is a dollar that can start working inside your **real Money Machine**—building assets, creating income, and compounding toward freedom instead of draining it.

The Three Financial Loops: Which One Are You In?

At any given moment, your money is in motion. Whether you realize it or not, it's flowing through a cycle—either one that keeps you stuck, one that keeps you comfortable but stagnant, or one that is actively moving you toward financial independence.

Most people don't stop to think about which cycle they're in. They work, spend, save a little if they can, and hope that someday they'll feel secure. But when you step back and look at the big picture, you can see that the way money moves through your life follows a pattern—a loop that repeats itself over and over again.

The good news? **Loops can be changed.**

Once you recognize which financial loop you're in, you can take intentional steps to shift into a better one. The goal is to move from survival mode to self-sufficiency, and ultimately to full financial freedom.

Let's break down the three financial loops so you can identify where you are—and where you want to be.

Loop 1: The Survival Cycle (The Debt Trap)

Earn → Cover expenses → Pay debt → No savings → Repeat.

This is where many people get stuck, living paycheck to paycheck with no financial cushion. Every dollar is accounted for before it even reaches their hands, and anything extra goes toward servicing debt rather than building wealth.

In this loop, bad debt becomes a **silent thief**, quietly stealing from your future. Credit cards, car loans, and high-interest personal loans may seem like solutions in the short term, but they keep you trapped in a cycle where past spending dictates your future choices.

Bad debt acts as a reverse Money Machine—it works against you, draining your future income through interest payments.

If your expenses consistently exceed your income, you're financing your lifestyle with debt. This might look like:

- Carrying credit card balances month after month.
- Taking out loans to cover everyday expenses.
- Living paycheck to paycheck with no buffer for unexpected costs.

It's easy to fall into this trap, especially in a society that normalizes living beyond our means. But the chart shows us why this doesn't work: when debt consumes your income, there's no money left for savings, and without savings, the Money Machine can't get started.

This isn't about shame or judgment—many people find themselves here due to circumstances beyond their control, like medical bills, job loss, or an unexpected crisis. The key is recognizing the problem and taking steps to reverse the flow.

How to break free:

- Reduce expenses aggressively to create breathing room.
- Focus on paying down high-interest debt as quickly as possible.

- Redirect even small amounts into savings to start changing the financial flow.

Every dollar that isn't spent on debt repayment is a dollar that can be directed toward financial security instead.

Loop 2: The Work-to-Spend Cycle (Stagnation Loop)

Earn → Cover expenses → Spend on lifestyle → Save a little, but not enough to reach financial independence.

This loop is where a lot of middle-class professionals get stuck. They're making enough to live comfortably—paying their bills, enjoying vacations, upgrading their lifestyle—but they aren't building true wealth.

In this loop, people *feel* financially stable because they're not drowning in debt, but they're also not making progress toward financial freedom. Savings exist, but they aren't being funneled into assets that will generate passive income.

The problem with this loop is that if the income stops, the lifestyle stops. There's no financial safety net beyond a savings account, and the ability to retire early, take a sabbatical, or step away from work is still out of reach.

How to break free:

- Shift your mindset from saving as a "rainy day fund" to saving as a tool for **investment**.

- Reduce unnecessary lifestyle expenses so that more money flows into savings.
- Commit to actively growing assets rather than letting money sit passively.

The key here isn't just cutting back—it's **making money work for you instead of letting it sit idle.**

Loop 3: The Freedom Cycle (Building the Money Machine)

Earn → Cover expenses → Save aggressively → Invest in assets → Assets generate income → Income covers expenses → Full freedom.

This is the **ideal loop** because it's the only one where money starts working for you instead of the other way around.

In this loop, savings are deliberately directed into **income-generating assets**—stocks, real estate, digital products, or profitable businesses. Over time, those assets generate enough income to cover basic expenses (Freedom Baseline) and eventually lifestyle expenses as well.

At this point, **you are no longer dependent on earned income.**

How to stay in this loop:

- Prioritize building passive income streams.
- Automate savings and investment contributions so money flows into assets consistently.
- Keep debt minimal to maintain flexibility and security.

This loop is where true financial independence happens. **At first, passive income covers the Freedom Baseline, but the long-term goal is for it to cover your entire lifestyle.**

The Role of the Money Machine: How to Break Free from Work Dependence

We already introduced the idea of covering your **Freedom Baseline** with passive income. This is the starting point because once that is in place your overall sense of financial safety will be huge which will also serve to expand your choices and freedom. However, true financial independence comes when passive income *also covers your lifestyle expenses.*

That's where the Money Machine comes in.

A **Money Machine** is built by directing savings into assets that create income. These can include:

- **Investment Accounts:** Stocks, bonds, index funds that grow over time.
- **Digital Products:** E-books, e-courses, and memberships that generate passive revenue.
- **Rental Properties:** Real estate that produces monthly cash flow.
- **Profitable Businesses:** Businesses that generate income without requiring your daily involvement.

The more you put into your Money Machine, the more it gives back—reducing your reliance on earned income.

Eventually, the goal is to **shift completely out of trading time for money** and let your Money Machine fund your ideal life.

Final Thoughts: Designing Your Personal Money Flow

The way money flows through your life isn't fixed—it's a design choice.

If you want financial freedom, you have to be intentional about where your money goes.

- **First, stop the leaks.** Reduce unnecessary spending, pay down debt, and control lifestyle inflation.
- **Next, shift savings toward assets.** The more you direct toward building your Money Machine, the faster you achieve freedom.
- **Finally, let your assets grow to cover more than just essentials.** The ultimate goal isn't just security—it's a life where **all** of your expenses are covered by passive income.

Where Do You Go from Here?

Now that we've mapped out how money moves, the next step is to actively build income streams that don't rely on your time.

In the next section, we'll explore exactly how to do that—through smart business and investment choices that allow you to step fully into financial freedom.

Because the goal isn't just to survive—it's to thrive, on your own terms.

My Money Machine: How I Designed a Life of Freedom

When I first started my business, I wasn't thinking about taking a three-year paid vacation. I wasn't dreaming of palm trees, island sunsets, or lazy afternoons by the pool. I was just trying to build security for my family, control over my time, and the ability to call the shots in my own life.

But that's exactly the point.

Financial freedom doesn't come from wishing for it. It comes from building the right systems, making smart choices, and being intentional about how money flows through your life.

When I realized I had done exactly that—that the Money Machine I had built could support me without having to trade my time for a paycheck—I had the incredible opportunity to step back. To pause, reflect, and actually enjoy the life I had been working so hard to create.

And so, I did something most people only dream about.

I moved to Bali with my kids.

And for three years, I lived completely off what's often called *passive income*. I prefer to think of it as *lower-maintenance income*—it still took planning and setup, but once the systems were built, the money flowed without my daily labor.

Raise Your Hand If You'd Like a Paid Three-Year Vacation

I know—that title might sound like clickbait. After all, who wouldn't want an extended, fully funded escape to a tropical island?

But this wasn't luck. And it wasn't about "taking a break" because I was burned out.

This was the payoff.

The moment I realized that everything I had been working toward—living below my means, reinvesting in assets, and prioritizing freedom over excess—had led me to exactly what I wanted: the ability to live life on my terms.

This was proof that the principles in this book work.

How I Built My Money Machine

The ability to step away from work for three years wasn't some magic windfall. It was the direct result of strategic decisions I had made years earlier.

I pieced together a system with three main components that became my Money Machine:

1. **Investment Accounts (The Safety Net)**
   I always made sure I had liquidity—accessible cash that provided security and peace of mind. I kept a portion of my savings in a high-interest account, so if anything unexpected happened, I had a cushion.

2. **Rental Properties (Steady Lower-Maintenance Income)**

   Real estate became an essential part of my Money Machine. While rental properties don't generate as much income as a thriving business, they require significantly less hands-on work. Over time, they appreciate in value, and rental income helps pay down the mortgage, increasing long-term wealth.

3. **Business Ownership (The Wealth Generator)**

   This was the foundation of it all. My business gave me an income, but more importantly, it gave me an asset—something that could be scaled, sold, or managed without my direct involvement.

I had designed a system where, even when I wasn't working, money was still flowing in. And when I combined that with a lower cost of living in Bali, the numbers worked effortlessly in my favor.

Designing a Life, Not Escaping One

Some people hear "three years in Bali" and assume I was running away. But the truth is, I wasn't escaping—I was finally fully living.

By 2011, I had been running my business for nearly a decade while raising two kids. I loved the independence and security it provided, but I also knew I wanted something more.

The 2008 financial crisis was a wake-up call. I saw so many friends in Silicon Valley—smart, capable professionals—lose jobs, homes, and financial stability overnight. It reinforced something I had already suspected: having a job is not the same as having security.

And yet, I wasn't the same woman who had left the corporate world a decade earlier. I had built something successful. I had options. And I realized that real freedom isn't just financial—it's the ability to step back and design your life with intention.

So instead of rebuilding the same life after the crash, I chose a new path.

I moved to Bali with my two children, where I could experience more, live more, and be more present—not just as a mother, but as a whole person.

A Freedom-Based Life for $3,500 a Month

Bali gave me time. And not just any time—high-quality, intentional, deeply fulfilling time with my children and myself.

For just $1,500 a month, I rented a stunning three-bedroom villa surrounded by lush greenery. It came with a pool, fruit trees, a full-time housekeeper, and a groundskeeper. I split the cost of a driver with another expat family, so I never had to worry about errands or logistics.

Here's the kicker: My cost of living was now dramatically lower than it had been in the U.S.

What struck me most wasn't just the beauty of the place—it was how much more alive I felt, simply because my cost of living was lower and my time was finally my own.

Because my Money Machine kept generating income, and because I was spending less, I had the ultimate luxury: freedom.

- My daughter attended an incredible international school nestled in the jungle.
- My three-year-old son spent his days barefoot, chasing dragonflies with Wayan, our housekeeper, who adored him.
- And for the first time in years, I had the time to breathe, reflect, and create.

I started writing again. I traveled with my kids, immersing us in new cultures and perspectives. I spent my days watching sunsets, learning new languages, and simply being.

And I wasn't working. Not because I didn't want to—but because I didn't have to.

More Than Just a Mom—More Than Just a Businesswoman

One of the biggest gifts of my time in Bali was rediscovering myself.

When I left the corporate world, I had created a strong two-legged stool: work and motherhood. But the third leg—me—was missing.

Bali reminded me that I mattered too.

And because I had outsourced the time-consuming daily tasks (laundry, cleaning, errands), I got to be fully present with my kids. Instead of being stuck in survival mode, I was able to experience life with them.

This wasn't just a vacation. It was a strategic pause—one that allowed me to return reenergized and more intentional than ever.

The Principles That Made It Possible

None of this happened by accident. They thought I was crazy again when I stepped back from my business and moved to Bali

1. **Live Below Your Means (And Save More Than You Think You Need)**
   When my business was thriving, I didn't let lifestyle inflation eat away my earnings. Instead, I saved aggressively and invested in additional income-generating assets.

2. **Make Your Money Work for You (Invest in Assets, Not Stuff)**
   I prioritized investments that produced income, like rental properties and private equity—not liabilities that drained money from my future.

3. **Reframe Money as a Tool for Freedom**
   My ultimate goal was never about "getting rich"—it was about creating a life where I had choice.

What Seems "Crazy" Today Might Be Your Reality Tomorrow

People thought I was insane when I left a high-paying corporate job to buy a hotel. They thought I was crazy again when I stepped back from my business and moved to Bali.

But every so-called "crazy" decision led me to freedom.

And that's what I want for you.

Not necessarily three years in Bali—but the ability to live life on your own terms.

Because the biggest flex isn't just financial success—it's having the freedom to step away and know that your Money Machine keeps working for you.

So if you're ready to start building your own, let's keep going.

Because this life? It's yours to design.

Exercise: An Invitation to Reimagine Freedom

Those three years in Bali taught me that freedom is about more than just financial security. It's about creating a life that aligns with your values, your dreams, and your family's needs. It's about knowing when to push forward and when to step back, giving yourself permission to rest without guilt and to pursue what makes you feel alive.

So ask yourself:

- What would your life look like if you had the time and space to breathe?
- What steps can you take today to start building that freedom for yourself and your family?

This is your chance to sketch your own version of Bali—whatever that looks like for you. The answer doesn't have to be a tropical island, but it does have to be yours.

Section III: Building Your Own Table

In Section I, we explored why a seat at someone else's table isn't enough—especially for moms who juggle multiple priorities in systems that don't always serve them. **In Section II**, we reframed how you think about work and money, introducing a *Business Freedom Mindset* that empowers you to take control of your future on your own terms.

Now it's time to translate that mindset into action. **Section III: Build Your Own Table** offers a practical blueprint for creating your own opportunities in the business world. We'll start by **Understanding Risk and Reward**—giving you the understanding of this fundamental relationship involved in all of business so you can decide where your comfort level is. Next, in **Choose Your Own Adventure**, you'll explore different types of business income so you can chart a path that aligns with your lifestyle and goals.

From there, **Starting a Business** looks at three women who created three very different types of businesses from scratch, while **Be the House** reveals how owning a business (rather than renting your talent to an employer) can shift you into the driver's seat of your financial future.

By the end of this section, you'll see how to *literally build your own table*: a place where you—and anyone you choose to invite—can thrive. In **Section IV**, we'll continue the journey with **You Don't Need an MBA, But You Do Need Skills**, delving into the concrete abilities you'll want to develop as you step into your role as the architect of your working life.

Let's begin. It's time to turn insight into action and lay the foundation for a life that works for you, not the other way around.

CHAPTER 8

Rethinking Risk

Most people assume that traditional jobs are safe and that entrepreneurship is risky. But is that really true? In most financial decisions, **risk and reward are inversely related**—meaning that higher-risk ventures often promise greater potential returns, while lower-risk options tend to offer limited upside. Based on that a job might be considered low risk and low reward compared to say starting your own business. However, risk isn't just about short-term stability—it's about control, adaptability, and long-term security.

A traditional job may *feel* stable because it provides a predictable paycheck and benefits. However, the trade-off is that your financial growth is largely dependent on external factors—your employer's success, market conditions, and company decisions that are outside of your control. On the other hand, investments and business ventures may seem riskier, but they offer a significant advantage: **control over your financial destiny and the potential for far greater long-term security.**

My own experience during COVID is a perfect example. When lockdowns hit in 2020, my hotel business faced a sudden and devastating loss of income. It was terrifying. I still had a mortgage to pay, but no guests were coming in. However, because I owned the business, I had the ability to pivot. I turned the hotel into temporary housing for individuals who needed to isolate due to age or health concerns. It didn't replace all the income I lost, but it kept the business afloat. Most importantly, it gave me agency in a situation where many others felt powerless.

This is the kind of control that solopreneurs and business owners can exercise—it doesn't eliminate risk, but it allows you to adapt, creating a unique form of safety in uncertain times.

This is why simply chasing what feels "safe" can backfire. **True security doesn't come from avoiding risk—it comes from understanding and managing it strategically.**

Rethinking What's Safe vs. Risky: How to Assess the Best Path for You

For most of us, the idea of "playing it safe" means **having a steady paycheck, a reliable job, and a clear financial path.** But is it really safe? Or is it just *familiar*?

True security isn't about where your paycheck comes from—it's about **having control over your income, options, and future.**

Think about it:

- If you lost your job tomorrow, how long could you sustain yourself?
- If your industry changed overnight, how would you adapt?

- If you had to take six months off for family or health reasons, would your income survive?

Many of us have been conditioned to believe that **working for someone else is the safest bet** when, in reality, relying on a single employer for income is one of the **riskiest financial positions to be in.**

To really understand risk, we need to rethink how we define it.

The Three Types of Risk (And How They Show Up in Your Finances)

Instead of thinking about risk as "risky vs. safe," let's break it down into three key categories. Every financial decision you make—whether it's choosing a career, starting a business, or investing—falls somewhere within these risk dynamics:

1. Short-Term vs. Long-Term Risk

A job provides an immediate and predictable paycheck. That feels safe. But what happens if you're laid off or your industry shifts? Over time, relying solely on a job can actually be riskier than building your own sources of income.

On the flip side, starting a business or investing in assets might feel riskier in the short term, because you're not seeing immediate financial returns. But in the long run, they offer far more stability and control.

Example: A salaried worker has a stable monthly income, but no financial safety net if the job disappears. A business owner, after a few years of effort, might have multiple income streams that continue paying them even if they step away.

2. Capital Risk vs. Employment Risk

There's a common fear that starting a business or investing is "risky" because it requires money upfront. But here's what often gets overlooked:

You're already taking a financial risk by depending entirely on your employer for income.

We call this employment risk—the danger of being fully reliant on someone else's decisions. If your company downsizes or your boss decides to replace you, you could lose 100% of your income overnight.

On the other hand, capital risk—like starting a business or buying an asset—means putting money into something uncertain, but with the potential to grow and work for you over time.

Key Takeaway: You're taking a risk either way. The real question is: Would you rather risk money to gain more control, or risk your financial future by leaving it in someone else's hands?

3. Control & Adaptability: The Key to Reducing Risk

The more control you have over your income, the less risky your financial position actually is.

- **A business owner can pivot and adapt**—shifting strategies, expanding services, or adjusting to market trends.
- **An investor can move money across different assets** to protect against downturns.
- **A job, on the other hand, gives you little control**—your income is tied to someone else's decisions.

When you take ownership of your income, you can adapt faster to economic changes. That's real security.

The Six Key Earning Paths (And Their True Risk Levels)

Instead of thinking about jobs, businesses, and investments as completely separate silos, let's reframe them as different strategies for **managing risk and control.**

Each of these six paths comes with its own balance of short-term vs. long-term risk, capital vs. employment risk, and levels of control. The key is to understand them so you can make informed choices.

---

1. Working a Job (Short-Term Safe, Long-Term Risky)

Best for: Immediate income, benefits, structured career growth.

Risk: No control over job security, dependent on employer.

A job provides **predictable paychecks and benefits,** but you have **zero control** over your financial future. If the company goes under or your position is eliminated, **your income stops immediately.**

Most people assume this is the safest path—but in reality, it's only safe **until it isn't.**

The best way to mitigate this risk is to start creating alternative income streams while you are working your job (what this book is about!)

2. Solopreneurship (Low Capital Risk, High Control, But Hard to Scale)

Best for: Freelancers, consultants, gig workers, service providers.

Risk: Income depends entirely on personal effort; no passive income.

Being a solopreneur gives you **flexibility and control,** but there's a catch: **if you stop working, your income stops too.**

This path is great for transitioning away from a job or creating financial stability, but it's still **trading time for money.** The next step is learning how to build something that works even when you don't.

3. Starting a Business (High Short-Term Risk, High Long-Term Security)

Best for: Those willing to build a long-term asset from scratch.

Risk: No guaranteed income at first, requires capital and effort.

Starting a business from the ground up **requires patience, risk tolerance, and resilience.** But once it's established, it can create exponential income growth, control, and financial independence.

This is **short-term risk for long-term gain.**

In my view this is the best option if you have a solid safety net – able to live at home for free with mom and dad or have a partner whose income completely covers your financial needs.

---

4. Buying a Business (Lower Risk Than Starting, More Control Than a Job)

Best for: People who want business ownership without the startup phase.

Risk: Requires upfront capital but offers immediate cash flow.

Instead of starting a business from scratch, you can **buy an existing business that's already making money.**

This path removes a lot of uncertainty—there's already a **proven customer base, revenue, and systems in place.** You're skipping the hard part and stepping into ownership **with cash flow from day one.**

I will show my bias here – this in my view is the best balance of risk and reward. You get income day one and the time freedom of being the boss. It's not risk free but nothing in life is!

---

5. Buying an Income-Generating Asset (Moderate Risk, Passive Income)

Best for: Those looking for semi-passive income streams.

Risk: Requires upfront investment, but creates long-term cash flow.

Rental properties, farmland, royalties, and even digital assets can provide **ongoing passive income.** While real estate values fluctuate, well-chosen assets **can provide steady cash flow with little ongoing work.**

The real issue here is that many of these sell at a high price relative to the income they provide and so unless you're starting with a lot of personal wealth it will be hard to generate enough income to cover your income initially – this is great though as a longer term play with less time commitment compared to owning a business.

---

6. Investing in Paper Assets (Market-Dependent, Low Control)

Best for: Long-term wealth-building, diversification.

Risk: No direct control over returns, subject to market shifts.

Investing in stocks, bonds, and index funds is a **passive way to build wealth** over time. But it's also the **least controllable.**

A market downturn can wipe out years of growth, and you have no way to influence the outcome. That's why **paper assets work best as part of a diversified income strategy, not the sole foundation of financial security.**

But the main advantage is they are the most liquid. You can sell them immediately compared to say real estate or businesses that can take months.

Final Takeaway: Which Risk Are You Willing to Take?

No path is 100% safe. But here are the key takeaways:

- Working a job might feel safe now, but it's long-term risky.
- Solopreneurship gives you control but can keep you stuck trading time for money.
- Business ownership and assets require upfront effort but provide lasting freedom.

The real risk isn't trying something new—it's staying in a situation where you have no control.

Now that we've reframed risk and security, let's take this a step further:

How do you actually build a portfolio of income streams that work for you?

That's what we'll dive into next.

Case Study: The Hidden Risk of "Playing It Safe"

When Sarah graduated from college, she did what she was taught was the responsible thing—she got a stable job with a $50,000 salary, contributed 10% of her paycheck into a 401(k), and planned for the future. She felt confident that she was making the "safe" choice.

Ten years later, she was laid off. The company restructured, and despite her loyalty and hard work, she found herself unemployed with limited savings. Her 401(k) had grown to $73,918, but with penalties for early withdrawal, it wasn't an immediate solution. She was stuck searching for another job, trading time for money all over again.

Now, let's compare Sarah to Lisa, who took a different path. Instead of relying solely on her job and a retirement account, Lisa decided to buy a small business for $100,000. She secured an SBA loan for $80,000 at 6% interest, putting down only $20,000 of her own money.

Her business steadily grew at 10% per year. After ten years, her business was worth $259,374, and she had paid down a significant portion of the loan. Her remaining loan balance was only $36,688, meaning her total business equity was now $222,686.

In other words, Lisa turned a $20,000 investment into over $220,000 in equity—more than 11 times her initial investment. Not only that, but she had a consistent income stream and never had to worry about being laid off.

Balancing Risk, Reward, Safety, and Freedom

Selecting the best path isn't about labeling one approach as universally "good" or "bad." Instead, it's about aligning your **risk tolerance, financial goals, and desired level of control** with a path that suits your life.

For example:

- **Prefer short-term paycheck stability?** A job might be best, though long-term freedom is limited.
- **Want faster independence without building from scratch?** Buying an existing business may offer the quickest path.
- **Crave ultimate freedom from daily involvement?** Investing in paper assets could work—if you're comfortable riding market ups and downs.

The secret is recognizing that **safety can mean different things**:

- **Short-term stability vs. long-term security**
- **Low capital risk vs. guaranteed paychecks**

Each option has trade-offs; understanding them is key to making informed decisions that fit your personal and financial aspirations.

Final Thought: Control is the Best Form of Security

Real security comes from **having multiple income sources and control over your financial future**. It's not about avoiding risk—

it's about managing and **strategically balancing** short-term and long-term security.

Sarah thought she was playing it safe, but when she lost her job, she had no backup plan. Lisa took on calculated risk, but in the end, she built a financial future where she called the shots.

So, what's your next move?

Exercise: Assess Your Risk Tolerance and Safety Nets

To decide where you want to be in the Freedom and Safety Matrix, it's important to understand your personal relationship with risk, reward, and control. This exercise will help you clarify your comfort level with uncertainty and identify the resources that can support you.

Step 1: Rate Your Comfort With Risk

On a scale of 1 to 10, rate your comfort with the following scenarios:

- Starting a business where success depends on your ability to find customers and manage operations.
- Putting your savings into an investment with the potential for high returns but also significant losses.
- Leaving a secure job for a freelance or solopreneur role with less predictable income.

Reflect on your answers: Are you naturally more risk-averse, or do you thrive on taking chances?

Step 2: Identify Your Safety Nets

Make a list of the safety nets you already have in place. For example:

- Do you have a spouse or partner with a steady income?
- Do you have savings that could support you for 6–12 months in case of a financial setback?
- Do you own a home or other assets that could be leveraged if needed?
- Do you have skills or experience that make you more adaptable in the job market?

Reflect on how these safety nets might impact your ability to take on risk. For example, having a financial cushion might make you more willing to pursue business ownership or investing.

Step 3: Consider Your Need for Control

Ask yourself:

- How much control do I want over my financial future?
- Am I comfortable relying on others (an employer, the stock market, etc.) for income, or do I prefer to create my own safety net?

Reflect on whether your need for control aligns with your current approach to earning and investing.

CHAPTER 9

Choose Your Own Adventure

In the previous chapter, we explored six different ways you could earn money—working a job, becoming a solopreneur, starting a business, buying a business, purchasing an income-generating asset, or investing in paper assets. It's an exciting range of possibilities, but it can also feel daunting. How do you choose which path is right for you?

Why You Might Need to Narrow the Options

Unless you already have significant capital in the bank—enough to live comfortably off the returns of your investments—paper assets or income-generating assets alone won't typically replace a full-time job. You'll still need another form of active income until you build those investments to a high enough level. That means, for most people, the real practical choices come down to:

- Working a Job
- Solopreneurship
- Starting a Business
- Buying a Business

Now, there's nothing wrong with a job or solopreneurship. Each has its pros and cons, and they might fit perfectly into the life you want to create. This book is about pursuing **authenticity**—listening to your heart and honoring the life you genuinely want. If that means thriving in a traditional career or enjoying the relative independence of being a solopreneur, own it. The key is to be purposeful in your choice, not default into a path that doesn't serve you.

Working a Job: When It Makes Perfect Sense

A job is often the most straightforward and stable route. You earn a steady paycheck with minimal personal risk. You may also:

- **Gain Experience on Someone Else's Dime**
  You get to learn valuable skills, test new ideas, and "make business mistakes" without risking your own capital. This can be especially beneficial early in your career.
- **Pursue Specialized Work**
  Some professions require the infrastructure of a larger organization—a hospital for a surgeon, a major tech company for an engineer, or a large production studio for certain artists. These roles often aren't easily replicated alone.
- **Love Your Work, Love Your Team**
  If you genuinely enjoy your job and find meaning in what you do, there is no need to feel pressured to change paths.

If this describes you, congratulations—you might already be living your best professional life. In that case, it makes sense to stick with simple, relatively low-maintenance investment options—like a mix of real estate, stocks, and bonds—to build additional security over time. That way, you're not trading even more hours for money. You're simply growing your nest egg gradually while you do the work you love.

Solopreneurship: Freedom with a Ceiling

Solopreneurship offers more flexibility and control than a traditional job—yet you'll still be trading your time for money. You can pick your clients, set your own rates, and work around your life's demands. This can be a fantastic option if you:

- **Want to Grow Slowly**
  If you're dipping your toes into entrepreneurship, freelancing or consulting can help you test the waters without a huge initial investment.
- **Only Need Supplemental Income**
  Maybe you're a part-time therapist, personal trainer, or designer. You enjoy the work, and it brings in additional cash while leaving you time to pursue family life, hobbies, or other passions.
- **Value Control Over Scale**
  You might love the personal interaction and craftsmanship of your service. You can shape a schedule that fits your lifestyle—even if it means your income remains tied to the hours you put in.

Solopreneurship can be fulfilling, but it rarely provides the time freedom that comes from decoupling your income from your direct labor unless you can do this part time and still make enough money to live. Many women find themselves "doing it all" as solopreneurs—marketing, bookkeeping, delivering services—leading to burnout if they ever want to earn significantly more.

The Time Freedom Dilemma: Trading Hours for Dollars

If this book's theme resonates with you—seeking time freedom—then you'll notice a persistent issue in both traditional jobs and solopreneurship: you're still exchanging your time for money, even if the amount or the environment is more flexible. Yes, you may earn a respectable living. You might even love your work. But at the end of the day, your income stops the moment you stop working.

This is where owning a business—whether you start or buy one—can change the game.

Starting vs. Buying a Business

For many, the real leap into time freedom and financial autonomy comes from having a self-sustaining business. That might mean scaling a small operation into a multi-person enterprise or acquiring an existing company with established cash flow. Let's briefly compare these two big options:

1. **Starting a Business**
   - You begin with a blank slate to create something truly your own.
   - You also face the uncertainty of building a customer base from scratch.

     ○   It can be hugely rewarding or incredibly challenging—often both.

2. **Buying a Business**
   - You acquire an existing operation, complete with established customers, processes, and revenue streams.
   - You'll need more capital at the outset, but it may be the *fastest and safest* way to replace your full-time income.
   - You skip much of the riskiest startup phase, though no business is ever guaranteed to succeed forever.

Either path can lead to genuine time freedom if you build (or maintain) systems that let the business run without your constant involvement. Imagine stepping away for a week (or a month) and still seeing your bank account fill up while you're gone. That's the real difference—your money is no longer purely tied to your hours.

Authenticity Over Aspirations

Ultimately, you should pursue the path that feels *right for you*, not the path you think you're "supposed" to choose. Here's a quick decision guide:

- **If You Love Your Field and Thrive on Structure:** A job may be perfect, with investments and income earning assets like a low touch long term rental on the side.

- **If You Crave Some Freedom but Don't Want Large Upfront Risk:** Solopreneurship can be a great middle ground.
- **If You're Ready to Build Something Big from Scratch:** Start a business and design it to scale beyond your direct labor.
- **If You Have (or Can Raise) Capital and Want Fast Track Income:** Buy a business with existing profits and systems in place.

The key is being intentional. Each choice brings trade-offs. Time freedom isn't for everyone. Some people genuinely enjoy their job or love the direct connection with clients they get as solopreneurs. And that's wonderful—this book's primary mission is to help you make decisions aligned with who you really are and the life you truly want.

For those who do yearn for time freedom and want to overcome the trap of trading hours for dollars, a deeper dive into buying or starting a business awaits you in the next chapter.

Real World Women, Real World Solutions

Hopefully, you remember the stories of Paula, Maria, and Abigail from Chapter 2. Each of their situations seemed hopeless and left them feeling trapped—yet they managed to find a path forward using the principles of this book. It's important to recognize that the courage and determination they summoned was neither quick nor easy. The time it took them to unravel their predicaments and rebuild their lives cannot be understated, nor should it be. Their journeys remind us that true transformation often happens slowly, one small step at a time.

Paula's Spanish Escape

For Paula, the high cost of London living and a demanding advertising career left her feeling disconnected from her kids. She wanted a life with fewer regrets, but she also couldn't just walk away from her financial obligations.

The Shift:

- **Rent Out the London Home**: Rather than selling her expensive property, Paula turned it into a rental, banking on London's strong real-estate market.
- **Relocate to Lower Costs**: Moving her family to southern Spain gave her a warmer climate, a slower pace of life, and significantly reduced expenses.
- **Part-Time Consulting**: While her rental income covered most of the family's needs, she dipped into solopreneurship by consulting remotely, leveraging her ad-agency experience for international clients.

The Outcome:

Now Paula can spend real time with her children—helping with homework, exploring local festivals, even strolling the beach at sunset. She discovered that embracing a creative income strategy (rent plus consulting) offered not only financial stability but also a magical quality of life she'd once only dreamed of.

Maria's Cleaning Collective

Maria arrived in the U.S. from Nicaragua on an asylum visa, juggling multiple low-paying jobs and rarely seeing her children. She was determined to learn English and find a better way, but it felt like she was always one paycheck away from disaster.

The Shift:

- **Build a Business**: Drawing on her improved English skills, Maria started her own cleaning service.
- **Empower the Community**: She hired friends from her Nicaraguan American community, giving them a safe landing spot while they built their language skills.
- **Focus on Client Satisfaction**: By handling customer acquisition and communications herself, she could secure better contracts and charge higher rates than she ever earned alone.

The Outcome:

With her cleaning collective thriving, Maria no longer needs multiple jobs. She's able to watch her children grow, attend their school events, and even take them on small weekend outings. Meanwhile, her friends have found a stepping stone to improve their English skills and earn fair wages. What started as a survival tactic turned into a sustainable business that lifts everyone up.

Abigail's Fresh Start

Abigail never planned on being a single mom, but when her marriage ended, she faced a stark choice: stay at home with no income, or dive headfirst into the workforce. She decided she wanted both enough money to support her family and the ability to be there for her kids in a meaningful way.

The Shift:

- **Move Back In with Parents**: Swallowing her pride, Abigail returned to her childhood home, giving herself a support system and childcare help.
- **Leverage Divorce Settlement**: She used the proceeds from selling her share of the family home to buy an existing tutoring business—one with a proven track record and immediate cash flow.
- **Earn More Than Teaching**: By owning the business, Abigail could set her hours, hire additional tutors, and scale as demand grew—all while being close to her kids.

The Outcome:

What felt embarrassing at first turned into a multigenerational bonding experience: her kids adore living with their grandparents, and Abigail has the emotional and logistical support she needs to rebuild her life. Meanwhile, her new tutoring venture provides a better salary than she earned as a teacher—enabling her to give her kids stability without sacrificing time with them.

One Goal, Many Paths

Whether it's relocating to a lower-cost country and renting out a primary home, starting a business that employs others, or purchasing an existing operation for instant income, these women found ways to integrate work, family, and financial security. Their solutions may not be yours—but they prove that when you dare to step outside the norm, **freedom, income, and motherhood** can all coexist more harmoniously than you ever imagined.

What If You Only Want a Little Extra?

Before we move on, it's worth acknowledging that you might be comfortable in your current role—job, solopreneur, or otherwise— and just want a bit more financial security. In that case, consider investing gradually in **income-generating assets** or **paper assets**— rental properties, REITs, index funds, or a conservative mix of bonds and equities. You won't get immediate big returns, but these can be great ways to grow your wealth over time without juggling another major venture.

Beyond This Book

While we'll touch on strategies for starting or buying a business, this book isn't a step-by-step manual for each path. Instead, think of it as a springboard—an invitation to expand your sense of possibility. In the appendix, you'll find resources and recommended readings for deeper dives into topics like small business acquisition, solopreneur tax structures, and more. For now, just know there's a world of proven tactics and experts out there to guide you once you pick your lane.

Next Chapter: Breaking Free from the Time Trap

Now that you've narrowed your options and considered which paths align with your vision, it's time to dig deeper into the biggest game-changers for time freedom: **buying or starting your own business**. In the next chapter, we'll explore how to make this leap, examine the financial metrics that matter, and share stories of women who took the plunge and never looked back. Whether you're driven by pure ambition or a desire for a more balanced life, understanding the essentials of business ownership can open doors you didn't even know existed.

Be the House

When my son was young, he was captivated by the glitzy casinos near our home. He saw the signs advertising huge jackpots and couldn't understand why I wasn't rushing inside to make our family rich.

One day, as we drove past, I invited him to really look: the flashing lights, the luxurious buildings, the endless crowds of people streaming in. Then I asked him: *How do you think the casino can afford all of that?*

That's when I explained a fundamental truth: the house always wins.

Casinos might occasionally hand out an eye-popping payout, but unlike their clients, casinos don't rely on luck. Every game is designed to favor the house over time. No matter how much individual players might win here and there, the odds are always tilted toward the casino. That's why the buildings shine, the lights flash, and the fountains flow—the odds are stacked in their favor.

I told my son: *It's always better to be the house.*

And this principle holds true for business ownership. The only reason a business can afford to pay you as an employee is because it's leveraging *your* work to make enough money to both pay you **and** profit for itself.

When you buy or start your own business, you become the house. You're no longer working only to enrich someone else—you're building something that benefits you in multiple ways. For working moms especially, this can mean creating both the safety and the freedom needed to balance work and family on your terms.

Here's why buying a business can be one of the best paths to achieving financial freedom.

Getting Paid Twice: Work and Ownership (and Eventually, a Third Time)

When you own a business, you're paid in two powerful ways. First, you can earn money for the work you do *in* the business—similar to the salary you'd take home at a traditional job. But beyond that, you also earn from owning the business itself—its profits, systems, and growth potential. That second stream is what makes ownership so powerful: your effort doesn't just generate a paycheck, it builds an asset that continues to pay you over time.

Think of it this way: as a solopreneur, or freelancer, even though you have the "freedom" of running your own business, you're still exchanging time for money. Every dollar you make still depends on your active involvement, and if you stop working, the income stops too. This setup can feel like freedom at first—no boss, no set schedule—but it doesn't provide true flexibility because the income stream isn't independent of your time. You're the engine, and without your direct effort, there's no movement.

A true business works differently because of systems. When you build processes, hire a team, and create ways for the business to function without your constant presence, you unlock what's sometimes called *leveraged income*. The business can generate revenue beyond your individual effort—because the value is created not just by you, but by the whole system you've built.

Think of a bakery. If you're the baker, you're up at dawn mixing dough and serving customers. But if you *own* a bakery, your recipes and brand live on through your team. Every pastry sold and every customer served contributes to your income—even if you're not behind the counter that day.

And here's another hidden advantage: ownership gives you built-in safety valves. If revenue dips or your family suddenly needs more cash, you can step back into the business, working more hours to increase your pay. You can also grow income creatively—launching new products, cutting unnecessary costs, or finding new markets. On the flip side, if you need more time freedom, you can hire someone to replace some of your hours. And if you've grown the business well, you may be able to step back without sacrificing income at all.

For working moms, this flexibility is game-changing. Your financial well-being isn't capped by a fixed salary, and your time isn't locked into someone else's schedule. You can expand or contract your role depending on what life demands, while the business itself continues to work for you. That's not just income—it's resilience, freedom, and peace of mind.

And here's the kicker: there's also a third payday that most people overlook. You can't "sell your job," but you *can* sell your business. Businesses are usually valued based on a multiple of the income they generate. For example, a small business that makes $80,000 a year might sell for about 2.5 times that number, or $200,000.

Let's walk it through simply:

- You buy that $200,000 business with an SBA loan, putting in 15% down—just $30,000 of your own money.
- The business pays you $80,000 a year in income while you own it.
- Over ten years, you finish paying off the loan and grow the business modestly so it's now worth about $325,000.
- When you sell, you walk away with that $325,000 in cash—*on top of* the income you earned all along.

In other words, you turned an initial $30,000 investment into ten years of steady income plus a final $325,000 payday at the end. That's the third way business ownership pays you: the sale of the asset itself.

In short, being an owner gives you access to the kind of income that isn't dependent on direct, constant effort. You're creating a foundation that benefits both you and your family, with the peace of mind that comes from knowing your financial security isn't resting solely on your shoulders.

Starting a Business — Three Stories, Three Paths

At this point, you understand why business ownership can be a game-changer: it gives you leveraged income, allows you to earn beyond your working hours, and puts you in control of your financial future. But not all businesses are structured the same way.

For many women, the idea of starting a business can feel overwhelming—especially if it conjures images of risky startups, venture capital, and years of financial uncertainty before turning a profit. But here's the good news: building a business doesn't have to mean reinventing the wheel or creating the next unicorn tech company.

In reality, most successful women entrepreneurs follow one of three distinct paths:

- **Starting Small & Lean** – A business built around an existing demand, often requiring minimal investment or overhead, that allows the owner to start making money quickly.
- **Solopreneur Upleveling** – A service-based or creative business that begins as a one-person operation but is then scaled through systems, automation, or a team.
- **True Entrepreneurship** – A more traditional startup model, where a woman brings a completely new concept to market, usually requiring larger financial investments and longer growth timelines.

While these paths share common principles, they each require different levels of risk, effort, and long-term vision. Let's explore real-life examples of how women have successfully navigated each of these approaches—starting with Jamie, who turned a simple but powerful idea into a thriving business that gave her the freedom and stability she needed.

---

1. Starting a Small Business — "Zoom Zoom Bowen"

For years, Jamie had built a life she loved as a wilderness educator, using nature as her classroom to teach kids resilience, teamwork, and curiosity. Her work was fulfilling, and combined with her husband's income, she found a comfortable balance between her passion for teaching and being present for her own two children.

But everything changed after the unexpected and devastating end to what she thought was their fairy tale marriage. With her children in tow, Jamie returned to her small hometown of Bowen Island, nestled off the coast of Vancouver. Being surrounded by family and old friends provided emotional support, but Bowen's charm as a tranquil island came with a downside—job opportunities were scarce.

As the sole caregiver to her children, Jamie faced mounting financial challenges. Determined to make ends meet, she learned some new skills and found seasonal gig work, sorting packages for the postal service during the holidays and even DJing local events. But the patchwork income wasn't enough. She needed a new plan—something more sustainable that could secure her family's future.

Bowen Island, with its stunning vistas and seasonal influx of visitors arriving by ferry, sparked an idea. Jamie noticed that while tourists poured onto the island each summer, there weren't many convenient options to explore the island beyond the ferry dock. Drawing on her experience traveling through countries where scooters were a cheap and environmentally friendly way to get around, Jamie envisioned a solution: **Zoom Zoom Bowen**—a scooter rental business to help visitors experience the island's beauty on their own terms.

Getting started wasn't easy. Jamie had minimal business experience and lacked the savings to invest. There were also some by-laws that needed to be changed in order to allow this kind of business on the island. Twelve people before her had tried and failed but she was determined, resourceful and unafraid to ask for help.

Once she succeeded getting the necessary legal changes in place she pitched her idea to a regional bank and secured a line of credit to purchase six scooters. To make it happen, she swallowed her pride and asked her parents to co-sign the loan. "It's okay to ask for help," Jamie reminds other women, "especially when it comes to building something for your family. You don't have to do it alone."

With a modest website and some word-of-mouth buzz, Jamie launched Zoom Zoom Bowen. That first summer, her scooters were nearly always booked, and by the end of the season, she turned a profit. The glowing reviews poured in, and reservations for the following year started rolling in before winter even ended.

Running a business as a single mom wasn't always easy. Summer days were long, with Jamie juggling bookings, maintenance, and logistics. But the freedom and flexibility of entrepreneurship allowed her to carve out moments of joy—playing on the beach with her kids between rental pickups or enjoying dinners together after a busy day.

Zoom Zoom Bowen became more than a business; it was a lifeline. It gave Jamie not only financial stability but also the confidence to chart a new path for her family. Her story is a testament to resilience, creativity, and the power of leaning on community support when needed. Jamie's journey shows that even when life throws you off course, it's possible to build something beautiful from the unexpected detours.

This first example highlights what I call the "start a small business" path—sometimes born out of a hobby or personal passion that grows into a thriving enterprise. It's not necessarily a tech startup or a massive product line, but it evolves beyond the initial, one-person operation into something bigger.

Jamie didn't just stumble into entrepreneurship; she built a real business by designing a system that could function independently. I know you may be thinking, wait a second, she was working by herself so why isn't she a solopreneur? There are three key factors that set *Zoom Zoom Bowen* apart from typical solopreneurship:

- **Automated Booking & Payments:** Instead of relying on phone calls or manual scheduling, Jamie invested in a website with an automatic booking system, ensuring her rentals could be reserved, processed, and paid for without her needing to be constantly involved.
- **Income That Wasn't Tied to Every Working Hour:** Once the scooters were rented out for the day, her job was essentially done—allowing her time to be with

her kids or focus on growing the business rather than constantly working for each dollar earned.

- **Scalability & Delegation:** While she handled rentals herself in the early days, Jamie structured the business in a way that allowed her to hire someone to manage rentals, check waivers, and hand out scooters. Unlike a solopreneur whose work relies on their personal skills or expertise, this was a business that could run without her direct involvement every day.

By spotting the unmet need for tourist transportation—especially on an island accessible only by ferry—Jamie created a service that quickly outperformed any traditional job available to her. Not only did *Zoom Zoom Bowen* provide a viable income stream, but it also gave Jamie far more flexibility and control over her time—exactly what she needed to support her children and rebuild her life on her own terms.

---

2. Solopreneur Upleveling — The Story of Chani Nicholas

Chani Nicholas didn't set out to build a media brand; she simply had a gift for reading birth charts and a passion for helping people understand themselves through astrology. In her early days, she offered one-on-one sessions from her living room, writing customized forecasts that quickly became so popular she could barely keep up with demand.

As word spread—partly through her own heartfelt blog posts and partly through enthusiastic client referrals—Chani found herself booked months in advance. The level of personal attention she gave each reading, while meaningful, left her with zero room to breathe. She was working non-stop, inching toward burnout, yet still turning people away.

That's when she made a pivotal decision: to take her business beyond its one-woman-show roots. Over time, Chani launched an astrology app that delivers daily personalized horoscopes for subscribers, allowing her to share her insights without having to personally write a new chart for every individual. She then created a line of journals, workbooks, and other tools that invite users to engage with astrology on a deeper, ongoing basis.

To support this expansion, Chani gradually built a team around her—customer service reps, marketing and tech experts, editorial staff, and more. What started as a lone solopreneur delivering individual sessions evolved into a thriving company of roughly **50 employees**, each playing a role in furthering Chani's mission to make astrology more accessible and empowering.

By leveraging technology and assembling a dedicated staff, Chani transformed her brand into a scalable venture. She remains the face and voice—her authenticity and personal touch are still the core of the business—but she's no longer the only person executing every task behind the scenes.

Why This Path Made Sense for Chani

Chani's story illustrates a classic solopreneur challenge: a beloved craft can become a bottleneck when demand grows faster than the hours in a day. Instead of remaining perpetually overbooked and overwhelmed, she chose to **scale** through digital platforms, products, and a strong team. This move not only freed her from the grueling "trading hours for dollars" routine but also allowed thousands more people to benefit from her astrological insights— proving that with the right strategy and support, a solopreneur can uplevel to something far greater than a one-person business.

3. True Entrepreneurship — The Story of heywell Beverage

Ashley Selman and Britt Dougherty first met at a Fortune 500 alcohol beverage company, drawn together in part by the experience of being two of the few women in a predominantly male corporate world. Both quick-witted and ambitious, they quickly discovered how much they had in common: a passion for brand strategy, a drive to excel, and an unshakable belief that health and wellness trends were the future of the beverage industry.

Year after year, they climbed the corporate ladder. By the time they found themselves in executive positions, they had not only formed a close friendship but also proven their ability to thrive in a tough, male-dominated environment. Still, something was missing. No matter how successful they were, they couldn't shake the sense that **their personal growth was limited in the corporate environment**.

A Growing Trend—and a Missed Opportunity

Ashley and Britt both saw a huge gap in the market: consumers were clamoring for their food and beverage to work harder, and younger consumers were drinking less alcohol. **There was a big white space for healthy, delicious functional beverages**, but their organization continued to focus only on alcohol.

Britt, in particular, had a personal passion for emerging functional wellness. Ashley and Britt liked the efficacy that ingredients like adaptogens provided but felt like the ingredients could be intimidating, were not convenient and they did not taste good. The more Britt and Ashley researched, the more they felt convinced that a modern, wellness-focused beverage brand could resonate with consumers far beyond the "healthy living" niche.

The Leap to Entrepreneurship

With their employer focused in a declining category facing turbulence —and with both women itching for a new challenge— Ashley and Britt decided it was time to strike out on their own. Their first step was brainstorming what they wanted this new brand to stand for: healthy delicious functionality made to help people meet the demands of modern life.

They named their emerging brand **heywell**—a friendly nudge to prioritize wellness in a hectic world. While the idea was crystal clear, the reality of starting a beverage company from scratch was daunting. Recipe development, ingredient sourcing, packaging design, distribution channels,—**the to-do list was endless**. And they knew they'd need serious financial backing to break into the competitive beverage industry.

Rallying Support and Raising Capital

Fortunately, both Ashley and Britt had **supportive husbands** who were willing to help provide a safety net during those early days. This cushion allowed them to devote time and resources to heywell without the constant fear of missing a mortgage payment. Still, they didn't want to rely solely on personal savings. Realizing the scope of their ambition, they decided to pursue venture capital (VC) funding.

Their combined track record in the beverage industry gave them credibility. They pitched a vision of a sleek, modern brand that would ride the wave of functional beverages—one poised to capture the attention of health-conscious millennials and beyond. After multiple rounds of meetings, they secured the backing they needed to launch at scale.

A Fresh Face in Functional Beverages

From there, heywell began to make waves in natural and special stores and online marketplaces. Each can was crafted to deliver specific benefits—stress relief, energy, or immune support—using adaptogenic herbs like ashwagandha and functional ingredients like L-theanine. Early customers loved the flavor and simplicity, and the brand developed a cult following.

It hasn't all been easy. Ashley and Britt have navigated supply chain disruptions, rapid scaling challenges, and an ever-evolving marketplace. Yet their shared commitment—and the knowledge that they **chose** this path for a more fulfilling and innovative life— keeps them driven. With each successful retail partnership and positive review, heywell cements its place as a rising star in the beverage world.

Why This Path Made Sense for Ashley and Britt

After excelling in a male-dominated corporate environment, Ashley and Britt found themselves at a professional ceiling. They had good jobs, but **no room to grow.** Leveraging their collective experience in the beverage industry, they seized an opportunity the market had ignored.

Their prior successes helped them raise VC funding, and their supportive husbands provided a buffer against the financial uncertainty of launching a startup. Although they face more risk and responsibility than they ever did in the Corporate world, **the reward is owning a brand that aligns perfectly with their vision**—and forging a path that redefines what "success" can look like for women entrepreneurs in the food and beverage industry.

Which Path Resonates With You?

These three stories illustrate different shades of what "starting a business" can look like:

Start a Small Business: It might begin as a hobby or niche service that organically grows into a profitable enterprise (Zoom Zoom Bowen).

Uplevel a Solopreneur Service: You start as the sole provider, then transition into products, apps, or team-driven service models (Chani Nicholas).

True Entrepreneurship: You identify a gap in the market and create something entirely new, potentially scaling rapidly with outside capital (heywell Beverage).

None of these approaches is easy, and all come with inherent risk. But the **payoff**—in the form of autonomy, creative fulfillment, and, hopefully, time freedom—can be enormous for the right person in the right circumstances.

A Note on Financial Realities

Starting a business—whether you're a solopreneur or a visionary founder—often means enduring a **slower** journey to break even or profit. This is why many women (myself included) opt to **buy** an existing business instead. When you purchase a business that already generates consistent cash flow, you leapfrog some of the riskiest, least profitable stages.

That said, if you're drawn to the creative challenge and personal satisfaction of building something entirely your own, these stories might spark ideas for you. If you're passionate about going from zero to fully functioning enterprise—and you have or can secure the runway to do it—don't let fear stop you. You might become the next Chani or the next heywell success story.

Coming Up Next: Buying a Business

If the startup route isn't for you—due to time constraints, financial requirements, or personal preference—you'll want to stick around for the next chapter. We'll explore buying a business as a direct path to achieving time freedom faster. From due diligence tips to the mindset shift required, you'll get a blueprint for avoiding some classic pitfalls and finding a business that aligns with your strengths.

Whichever path you choose, remember the core message: there is no single "right" way. Whether you're forging a brand-new market concept, slowly scaling a solopreneur venture, or purchasing an existing enterprise, your journey should reflect your passions, financial reality, and the lifestyle you're aiming to create.

CHAPTER 11

The Advantage of Buying Cash Flow Up Front

Buying a Business: The Shortcut to Cash Flow

One of the biggest advantages of buying an established business is that you're purchasing something that's already making money. This is what we mean by "buying cash flow." Instead of starting from zero and hoping to build a profitable business over time, you're stepping into a setup that's already generating income.

This existing cash flow is like the steady income you'd get from a job—except it's generated by the business itself, not just your own labor. And unlike a paycheck, which disappears as soon as you stop working, the business cash flow keeps running, working as a financial engine that can support you and your family.

The Shortcut to Profitability: Why Buying Is Different from Starting

Think of two women—Lisa and Rachel—who both dream of owning a boutique fitness studio.

- **Lisa the Startup Founder** leases a space, spends months securing permits, hires instructors, and launches a marketing campaign. The first year is brutal—she's barely breaking even, relying on savings, and spending long hours in the studio to make it work. Three years later, she's profitable but exhausted.
- **Rachel the Business Buyer** takes a different approach. Instead of starting from scratch, she buys an existing fitness studio with a loyal customer base and a track record of profitability. From day one, revenue is flowing in, covering expenses, paying her a salary, and allowing her to focus on expansion instead of survival.

Rachel didn't buy a business idea—she bought cash flow. She stepped into a system that was already working and skipped the struggle phase. That's the power of buying instead of building.

Be the House: Why Owning the System Matters

In terms of the "house always wins" analogy, imagine buying a casino that's already operational. The games are running, customers are coming in, and the cash registers are ringing. When you buy the casino, you're not just acquiring the physical space— you're acquiring the cash flow it generates.

You don't have to spend years building brand awareness, perfecting processes, or finding your first customers. You're stepping into a business where the demand, revenue, and profitability have already been established.

For working moms, buying cash flow upfront is a game-changer because it minimizes risk and provides stability.

No Guesswork – Unlike a startup, where you cross your fingers that people will buy, an established business already has paying customers.

Immediate Paycheck – You're not burning through savings; you have an immediate income stream.

Faster Path to Hiring Help – You can afford to delegate sooner, reducing overwhelm and creating more balance.

When you own the house, you're not relying on someone else's payroll for financial security—you're creating it for yourself.

Using the Business as a Money Machine

Just like personal savings gives you the fuel to invest and grow, reinvesting business profits is what turns an ordinary company into a Money Machine. If you spend every dollar your business makes, the growth stops with you. But when you set aside a portion of the profits and channel them back into the business, you create a cycle where money multiplies instead of stalls.

This is one of the most overlooked advantages of ownership. A paycheck only covers today's bills, but a business allows you to reinvest in tomorrow's income. The Money Machine doesn't just run because you own a business—it runs because you feed it with smart, intentional reinvestments.

How Profits Can Be Reinvested for Growth

Just like spending less than you make personally creates savings that fuel income generation, reinvesting some of your business profits helps the business grow and ultimately generate more income. This can include:

Marketing for Expansion – Running ads, adding new services, building a referral program, or launching an online store.

Upgrading Operations – Automating systems, improving equipment, or streamlining processes to increase efficiency and profitability.

Paying Yourself Strategically – Taking profits in smarter ways, rather than as a high-taxed salary, allows more of your money to keep working inside the business.

Here's a personal example. At the hotel I once owned, the business made about $100,000 more than I needed to live on in a given year. I had a choice: I could take that extra money as income, pay about 20% in taxes, and net $80,000—or I could reinvest it back into the business. I chose reinvestment. I upgraded the rooms and raised the average daily rate by just $15. With 28 rooms running at 70% occupancy, that small increase added **$107,310 in extra annual revenue.**

The best part? I made back my entire investment in the first year. And in every year after, that $107,000 flowed in as additional profit. But the benefit didn't stop there. Because businesses are valued on a multiple of earnings, that recurring revenue also boosted the future sale price. At a modest 2.5x multiple, the business gained **$268,000 in additional value**—on top of the yearly cash flow.

That's the Money Machine in action. By reinvesting strategically, you don't just protect your profits from taxes—you grow them into something bigger, stronger, and more valuable.

A Rare Combination of Safety and Freedom

At first, when you buy a business, you'll likely be deeply involved in its operations. But the real goal isn't to own a job—it's to own a system.

The difference? A job depends on your time. A system makes money whether you're there or not.

But here's something equally important: a business gives you the ability to step back in if you need to. Unlike a traditional job, where layoffs or industry downturns can wipe out your income overnight, owning a business gives you a fallback option. If revenue dips or your family suddenly needs more cash, you can roll up your sleeves, step into the business, and directly influence the outcome.

That's a level of safety most jobs don't offer. With a paycheck, you're at the mercy of someone else's decisions. With a business, you have levers you can pull: take on more client work, launch a new service, tighten expenses, or temporarily take on a role yourself. You have agency.

And then there's the freedom side. If your priority shifts—say you need more time at home, or you want to step back to focus on health, family, or travel—you can hire staff to cover your role. Yes, you may earn a little less in the short term, but unlike a paycheck, the business doesn't collapse when you step away. If you've grown it well, the system itself keeps humming.

For many moms, this combination is revolutionary. You're not locked into an all-or-nothing choice between safety and freedom. You get both: the security of knowing you can always step back in, and the freedom of knowing you don't have to. That's what makes business ownership so appealing—it creates a foundation flexible enough to hold both your family and your future.

Why Buying a Business Beats Buying Real Estate

Many people consider real estate a great way to generate passive income—and it can be. But for most people, building enough passive income through real estate to replace a full-time salary takes years—sometimes decades. You have to save up for down payments, build equity slowly, and accumulate multiple properties before the cash flow becomes meaningful.

Buying a business, on the other hand, can often allow you to replace your job income immediately. Instead of waiting years for rental properties to generate enough cash flow, a profitable business provides immediate income from day one.

One of the simplest ways to compare investments is by looking at how much income they produce for every dollar you put in. Think of it like this: if you invest $300,000, how much yearly income can you expect back?

Rental Property Example: On average, rental properties return about **4–6%** a year. That means if you buy a $300,000 property, you might earn **$12,000 to $18,000 per year** after expenses. That's nice extra money, but it's not nearly enough to replace a full-time salary.

Small Business Example: Most small businesses sell at returns closer to **15–25%**. Using that same $300,000, you could earn **$45,000 to $75,000 per year**. That's three to four times more than a rental property and puts you much closer to covering—or even replacing—a paycheck.

And here's what makes business ownership even more powerful: with a rental property, you're at the mercy of the market and local rent prices. With a business, you have levers you can actually pull to increase income. You can add new products, raise prices, cut costs, or expand into new markets. That means your return isn't just passive—it's something you can actively grow.

And before you panic at the idea of needing $300,000 in cash—don't worry. In the next chapter, we'll talk about how to buy a business for a fraction of the purchase price using leverage. It's not only possible—it's the way most entrepreneurs do it.

Wait, Aren't I Just Hiring Other Women to Work for Me?

It's a fair question: "If I buy a business, am I just creating more trading-time-for-money jobs for other women while I take the profits?"

Here's the truth: **work itself isn't the enemy.** What's harmful are jobs that don't pay fairly, lack flexibility, or treat people as replaceable.

The reality is that people need and want different things at different stages of life. Some thrive on the stability of a paycheck. Some want a part-time job that flexes around school drop-offs and soccer games. Others want to grow in their careers without carrying the risks of ownership.

The goal isn't to eliminate employment—it's to create *good* employment. When you own a business, you have the chance to design jobs that reflect your values.

In my own businesses, I hired moms who needed flexible schedules. Sometimes they even brought their kids to work when childcare fell through. Instead of being penalized, they were supported. That's the difference between just giving someone a paycheck and creating real opportunity.

And here's something even more powerful: by showing women— even the ones who work for you—what ownership looks like, you plant the idea that they can do it too. Many women have never seen business ownership up close. By mentoring or modeling what's possible, you may be giving someone the confidence and tools to make the leap themselves one day.

So no—you're not exploiting others to buy your freedom. **You're modeling a better way of working.** By owning a business, you get to shape a workplace that works for everyone: one that sustains you, uplifts your team, and maybe even launches the next generation of women business owners.

Gary's Leap: Leveraging Stability Into Opportunity

Wait—Gary? Isn't this a book for working moms? Yes, it is. But financial freedom and the tension between work and caregiving aren't just "women's issues." Many dads are also the primary parent, and they wrestle with the same unholy compromise of earning an income while being present for their families. Gary's story shows that the principles of ownership and financial resilience aren't gendered—they're human.

Gary had always been a loyal and dependable employee. For over two decades, he worked for a mid-sized company, earning a stable income that allowed him to live comfortably. While he wasn't living extravagantly, Gary had made smart decisions along the way— like buying a modest condo in his thirties, which he managed to pay off within 15 years. Though he sometimes envied the larger, flashier homes he saw on his way to work, his condo's low cost of living gave him something even more valuable: peace of mind. Gary often thought about how soundly he slept, knowing he had no mortgage hanging over his head.

That peace was shaken when his company announced plans to move its operations overseas. For the first time in years, Gary felt vulnerable. He was in his early fifties, an age where he worried he might face challenges competing in the job market, even with his excellent skills. The idea of starting over in a new job with a new boss felt exhausting and uncertain. "What happens," he wondered, "if I can't find something else?"

Gary was also the primary parent for his son, and the thought of losing both stability and flexibility was daunting. Around this time, he attended a local community talk about creating income-generating assets. The speaker discussed the concept of buying businesses instead of starting one from scratch, pointing out that many small business owners were looking to retire and sell. Gary had never considered business ownership before, but the idea intrigued him. He liked the thought of having more control over his income and schedule while building something for himself instead of working for someone else.

That night, Gary went down an internet rabbit hole. He began browsing websites listing businesses for sale in his area, curious about what was out there. One listing caught his attention: a water purification company. It was only about 20 minutes from his condo, and the current owner was looking to retire. Even better, the business already had a team in place to handle the technical aspects of installations. Gary realized he wouldn't need to become an expert in water systems—his role would focus on managing the team, sales, and marketing, which aligned with his skills.

The numbers looked promising. The asking price for the business was $220,000, and it generated $120,000 annually for the owner. Gary did the math: even with a loan payment, the business could provide him with a significant income—more than he was making at his current job. It seemed almost too good to be true.

The biggest hurdle was how to finance the purchase. Gary didn't have $220,000 sitting in savings, but he was determined to make it work. After some research, he decided to do a cash-out refinance on his condo to access the $22,000 needed for a 10% down payment. He applied for an SBA (Small Business Administration) loan to cover the rest of the purchase price. It felt like a bold move—

leveraging his home to buy a business—but Gary believed in the opportunity.

The transition wasn't without its challenges. There were forms to fill out, meetings with the bank, and a steep learning curve as Gary got up to speed on the business operations. But by the time he officially took over, he felt a mix of pride and relief. He had done it—he had bet on himself.

The results were life-changing. After the debt payment, Gary was bringing home over $90,000 annually—$20,000 more than he had been earning at his old job. And perhaps even more valuable was the lifestyle shift. Gary only needed to work about 30 hours a week, and he could do much of his work from home. No more long commutes to the office or rigid 9-to-5 schedules. On Wednesdays and Fridays, he enjoyed a slower morning, sipping coffee on his balcony before starting his day. He even had time to join a local hiking group, something he had always wanted to do but never had the flexibility for.

Reflecting on his journey, Gary realized how his earlier decisions—like living modestly and paying off his condo—had set the stage for this opportunity. By keeping his freedom baseline low and avoiding bad debt, he had built a foundation that allowed him to take this leap when the time came.

Gary's story is a powerful reminder that financial freedom isn't just about making more money—it's about making smart choices with the resources you have. By turning his stability into opportunity, Gary not only secured his financial future but also gained the flexibility and lifestyle he had always dreamed of.

And while this book is written for moms, it's important not to make gender assumptions about the unholy compromise of parenting and working. Many dads, like Gary, also want and need more freedom and safety. For moms, that matters too—because when men step into this conversation, it helps shift cultural norms and workplace expectations. Flexible, freedom-based models of work stop being seen as "special accommodations" for women and start being understood as better systems for everyone.

The takeaway? Building a Money Machine isn't just a mom's strategy—it's a family strategy. And when more parents embrace it, everyone benefits.

Final Thoughts: Owning Your Future

The goal of buying your own business isn't just to make money—it's to create a life where you have control over both your financial security and your time. This is about owning your future and designing it in a way that truly works for you and your family. In a world where many working moms are stretched thin, juggling responsibilities and feeling torn between work and family, owning a business offers a unique blend of freedom and security.

By stepping into ownership, you're choosing to be the house. You're choosing to stop trading time for someone else's profit and instead build something that benefits you on multiple levels. You're creating a life where financial stability, time freedom, and personal fulfillment are not competing interests but rather complementary goals.

Section IV:
You Don't Need an MBA but You Do Need Skills

Hopefully, by now, you're starting to think differently about money, freedom, and security. Maybe you're reimagining what life could look like if your time wasn't always tied to a paycheck — if your money could work for you, instead of the other way around.

It all sounds great, right? The dream of stepping off the hamster wheel, building financial security, and carving out time for what really matters. But let's be real: you've probably read this kind of thing before.

You've seen the books and heard the podcasts that light a fire under you — convincing you that financial freedom is just one bold leap away. Yet when it comes time to make a move, you're left thinking, "But how do I actually do that?"

This is where things often fall apart. The theory sounds inspiring, but the practical steps feel out of reach — confusing, overwhelming, or just plain intimidating.

That's why this section exists.

It's time to get practical. I'm not here to give you generic advice about 'following your passion' or 'manifesting abundance.' We're going to talk about the real skills you need to own or buy a business — skills that don't require an MBA, a million-dollar trust fund, or a shark tank full of investors.

We'll break down the essentials, step by step, so you can make informed, confident decisions. We'll talk about evaluating business opportunities, understanding key financial terms, managing risk, and most importantly, knowing what makes a business worth your time and money.

Because let's be honest: Freedom isn't free. It requires strategy, knowledge, and the willingness to take action. This is where that journey begins — turning ideas into action and excitement into opportunity.

Ready? Let's get to work.

CHAPTER 12

Why You Can't Buy a Million-Dollar Home But You Can Buy a Million-Dollar Business

Now that you have some savings you might be starting to think about what kind of business you can buy. Before I bought my first business, I thought only a rich person could afford to buy one. I imagined business ownership was reserved for people with deep pockets, vast savings, and endless financial resources. After all, I couldn't imagine walking into a bank and getting a loan for a million-dollar home. So, how could I ever afford a hotel with a similar price tag?

The idea seemed outlandish, almost laughable. I was thinking the way most people do—that buying a million-dollar property of any kind requires a million dollars, or at least a personal income to qualify for that much debt. But I learned something that turned my entire perspective upside down: when it comes to buying a cash-flowing business, the financing works very differently. Unlike a home, where banks rely on your personal income to determine if you qualify, buying a business is actually based on the **business's own ability to generate income**.

This difference is powerful. It means you don't have to be "rich" to buy a business. You don't need an extravagant salary or massive savings. Instead, what matters is the **cash flow of the business**—its ability to make money and pay for itself. Once I realized that, the doors to business ownership opened up in a way I never expected.

In this chapter, we're going to break down why buying a business is so different from buying a personal asset like a home. We'll look at the financial factors that make business ownership possible and explore the role of leverage—using other people's money (in this case, the bank's) to take control of a cash-flowing asset that can grow in value over time. And by the end of this chapter, you'll see that buying a business isn't about being wealthy; it's about understanding how to make your money work for you.

The Difference Between Buying a Home and Buying a Business

Let's start with the basics. When you buy a home, the bank wants to know one thing: can you afford the mortgage? They look at your salary, your personal savings, and your debt-to-income ratio. The loan is based on **your ability to pay** out of your own income, because the home itself doesn't generate cash flow. In fact, it's the opposite—owning a home typically means ongoing costs like property taxes, maintenance, and insurance. If your income suddenly stopped, you could struggle to keep up with these payments.

Buying a business, on the other hand, is entirely different. A business is a **cash-flowing asset**—it generates income. When you apply for a loan to buy a business, the bank doesn't focus as much on your salary. Instead, they look at the **business's cash flow**. They want to know if the business can produce enough money each month to cover its own expenses, including the loan payments. Essentially, the loan is based on **the business's ability to pay for itself**.

This distinction changes everything. You don't need to be a high-income earner to buy a business; you just need to find a business that can cover its costs and make enough profit to pay off the loan. The *business's* income qualifies it for the loan—not your personal wealth. This means that a million-dollar business might be well within your reach, even if a million-dollar home isn't.

A Tale of Two Purchases: House vs. Small Business

Let's be honest a million dollar anything might seem far-fetched and out of reach for most women. Let's see however how these two options stack up using some real-world numbers as an example.

Meet Sarah, a hardworking professional earning around $50,000 per year. She has her sights set on buying a home in a pleasant neighborhood but keeps running into a familiar hurdle: lenders say her income simply doesn't meet the mortgage requirements for the house she wants.

Trying to Buy a $400,000 Home

Sarah finds a cozy, two-bedroom house listed for **$400,000**. Here's what the bank tells her:

- **Purchase Price:** $400,000
- **Down Payment (20%):** $80,000
- **Loan Amount:** $320,000
- **Interest Rate (30-Year Fixed):** ~6%
- **Monthly Principal & Interest:** ~$1,920
- **Taxes & Insurance:** ~$300–$400 per month

All in, her monthly payment hovers around **$2,300**.

Debt-to-Income (DTI) Roadblock

A typical **Debt-to-Income (DTI)** limit for a residential mortgage is roughly **43%**. That means your total monthly debt payments shouldn't exceed 43% of your gross monthly income. To afford $2,300 per month under that guideline, Sarah would need:

- **$2,300 ÷ 0.43 ≈ $5,350** in gross monthly income
- This translates to around **$64,200** annually

Sarah earns $50,000 a year, and she has a small student loan on top of that. As a result, her DTI exceeds the lender's threshold, leading to a **denial** for the home mortgage.

A Different Path: Buying a $400,000 Laundromat

Still determined, Sarah shifts her attention to a small laundromat for sale nearby. The asking price is **$400,000**, which includes both the business and the property itself—making it eligible for an **SBA loan**. She investigates further:

- **Purchase Price:** $400,000
- **Down Payment (SBA):** 10% ($40,000)
- **Loan Amount:** $360,000
- **Interest Rate & Term (SBA 7(a)):** ~6–7% over 25 years
- **Monthly Principal & Interest:** ~$2,300

Key Difference: Cash Flow

Unlike a single-family home that *consumes* cash each month, the laundromat *generates* income. Suppose it's netting around **$3,500** per month after covering operating expenses (utilities, supplies, minor repairs, etc.).

- **Monthly Net Operating Income (NOI):** $3,500

That's **$42,000** per year ($3,500 x 12), giving the property:

- **Cap Rate:** $42,000 ÷ $400,000 = **10.5%**

This figure is within a reasonable range for a small business property with real estate included.

Debt Service Coverage Ratio (DSCR)

The SBA typically wants to see a **DSCR of at least 1.25**. That means the business should generate at least 25% more net income than the loan payment requires.

- **Monthly Loan Payment:** ~$2,300
- **Monthly Net Income:** $3,500

DSCR = $3,500 ÷ $2,300 ≈ **1.52**

A DSCR of 1.52 is comfortably above 1.25, indicating there's a healthy buffer to cover the loan payment.

In addition, this loan is guaranteed by the SBA. That means the lender is willing to take a risk on what might otherwise be considered too risky for them because the government will cover their losses in case of default.

Sarah's small business loan is **approved**!

Easier to Manage Than You'd Think

Another advantage for Sarah is that a laundromat can be relatively easy to run. She could:

- Keep her **day job** and oversee the laundromat's operations part-time.
- Hire a part-time attendant or use self-service machines, minimizing day-to-day labor requirements.

With the business covering its own loan payment—and leaving a surplus—Sarah effectively adds another income stream to her household.

Why the Bank Says "Yes" to the Business

For a House:

- The lender looks at *Sarah's personal income* and calculates a (Debt to Income) DTI ratio that exceeds their limit.
- She is denied a $400,000 mortgage because she doesn't meet the income threshold.

For the Laundromat:

- The lender focuses on the *business's cash flow* and its capacity to repay the loan (DSCR of 1.25+).
- At a $3,500 monthly net, the laundromat more than covers its $2,300 loan payment.
- The SBA also requires less money down* (10% vs. 20%), making the upfront cost more manageable.

The Takeaway

Sarah's story illustrates the dramatic difference between buying a **cash-flowing asset** (the laundromat) versus buying a **single-family home** (an expense). While she didn't qualify for a standard $400,000 home mortgage, she could successfully purchase a $400,000 business property because its *own* income stream provides the lender with enough confidence in repayment.

- **Lower Down Payment:** 10% vs. 20%
- **Comfortable DSCR:** 1.52 (above SBA's 1.25 minimum)
- **Extra Income Each Month:** Even after loan payments, the laundromat provides surplus cash

This example shows you don't need a six-figure salary to finance a sizable purchase; you just need a deal where the *asset pays for itself*.

*the SBA can require up to 20% down but 10% is the minimum it will depend on credit worthiness and experience of the buyer, strength of the business and the industry.

The Power of Leverage: Why Using Debt is Smart for Business Purchases

One of the scariest words in finance is "debt," and for good reason. Most of us are taught to avoid debt as much as possible. I even warned you about it in the previous chapter as it creates a "negative money machine." But here's the thing: when used correctly, debt can be a powerful tool—especially when it comes to buying a business. In fact, using leverage (debt) to buy a business is often safer than using debt to buy a home, because the business itself is designed to generate the cash flow needed to pay off that debt.

When you finance a business purchase, the bank typically covers **80-90% of the cost**, while you're responsible for the remaining 10-20%. In this case, the bank is actually taking on most of the financial risk. Since they're putting up most of the money, they're very careful about which businesses they'll finance. Banks don't want to risk a loss, so they scrutinize every aspect of the business's financials before approving the loan. They look at the cash flow, the industry, and the business's stability to make sure it's a sound investment.

In other words, **the bank acts as a sophisticated vetter**, doing thorough due diligence to determine whether the business is financially viable. If they're willing to finance it, that's a strong indication that the business can produce enough income to cover its costs, including the loan payments. The bank's willingness to finance a business isn't just a stamp of approval; it's a sign that they believe in the business's potential to succeed. By utilizing the bank's loan, you're able to control a large, valuable asset with minimal personal risk.

Compare that to a mortgage on a million-dollar home. When you take out a mortgage, you're fully responsible for the loan payments, and you're relying solely on your personal income to cover them. If you lose your job or face a financial emergency, you could be left scrambling to make ends meet. But with a business loan, you have the business's cash flow to rely on—not just your own paycheck.

Why Leveraged Returns Are So Powerful

Let's dig into the numbers to see why using leverage can be incredibly powerful and why this book is more about buying a business than teaching you investing skills. Imagine you have $400,000 that you want to invest. You could put that money into the stock market, or you could use it as a down payment to buy a cash-flowing business.

1. **Investing in the Stock Market**: If you invest $400,000 in the stock market, and it grows by 10%, you'll gain $40,000. That's a decent return, giving you a **10% return on your investment**.

2. **Buying a Business with Leverage**: Now, let's say you use that same $400,000 as a 20% down payment on a $2 million business, with the bank financing the remaining 80%. If the business grows by 10% in value (the same amount the stock market investment grew at), its cash flow increases by $200,000. But here's the kicker: because you only invested $400,000 of your own money, that $200,000 gain represents a **50% return on your initial investment**.

Here's how the math works out:

- In the stock market, a 10% gain on your $400,000 investment yields a $40,000 return—a 10% ROI.
- With the leveraged business purchase, that same 10% growth on the $2 million business yields a $200,000 return, **giving you a 50% ROI** on your $400,000 down payment.

This is the magic of leverage. By using a bank loan to control a larger asset, you're able to amplify your returns significantly. The bank's loan allows you to take ownership of the entire business and benefit from its full growth potential, even though you only put down a fraction of the purchase price.

Get the Seller to Help You Buy

Most people assume that to buy a business, you need to come up with a massive down payment and secure traditional financing for the rest. But what if I told you that **the seller can actually help finance your purchase**—allowing you to get in with less money down, better cash flow, and a built-in safety net?

One of the most powerful yet underutilized financing strategies is asking the **seller to carry a subordinated second loan**, structured as interest-only for five years. This arrangement benefits both the buyer and the seller in ways that might not be obvious at first glance.

How Seller Financing Works

Here's how structuring a **seller-financed second loan** can set you up for success:

- **Lower Down Payment:** Instead of needing a huge chunk of cash upfront, a seller-financed second loan allows you to get into the business with **less money out of pocket**.
- **Stronger Cash Flow:** Because the seller note is **interest-only**, your payments in the first few years are lower, keeping more cash in the business when you need it most.
- **Refinance for Better Terms Later:** After **two years of tax returns** under your ownership, you can refinance the seller note into a **traditional bank loan**, often at better terms, once you've built a stronger financial history.

- **Time to Learn & Grow:** The structure **buys you time** to learn the business, optimize operations, and **increase its value** before taking on a higher debt burden.

Let's Compare Two Deals

To see why seller financing can dramatically change the outcome of a purchase, let's compare two ways to buy the same $1,000,000 business.

For simplicity, we'll assume:

- SBA loan term: 10 years
- Interest rate: 10%
- Seller note: interest-only for 5 years at 6%

(These numbers are illustrative — the goal is to understand structure, not predict exact rates.)

Scenario 1: SBA Loan + Seller-Financed Second Note

(Optimizing Cash Flow)

Instead of using an SBA loan for the full 90% of the purchase price, you negotiate with the seller to carry part of the price as a second loan.

This reduces the size of your SBA loan and lowers your monthly payments during the most fragile years of ownership.

Purchase Price: $1,000,000

- Buyer Down Payment (10%): $100,000
- SBA Loan (First Position): $700,000
- Seller-Financed Note (Second Position): $200,000 (*interest-only for 5 years*)

Monthly Debt Payments

- SBA loan payment (10 years @ 10% on $700,000): ≈ **$9,250 / month**
- Seller note payment (interest-only @ 6% on $200,000): ≈ **$1,000 / month**

Total monthly debt payment: ≈ **$10,250 per month**

This structure gives you room to learn the business, stabilize operations, and build reserves — instead of drowning in debt from day one.

Scenario 2: SBA Loan Only

(No Seller Financing)

If the seller won't finance part of the deal, you must rely on an SBA loan for the full 90% of the purchase price.

Purchase Price: $1,000,000

- Buyer Down Payment (10%): $100,000
- SBA Loan (First Position): $900,000

Monthly Debt Payments

SBA loan payment (10 years @ 10% on $900,000): ≈ $11,900 per month

Because the entire loan is fully amortized from day one, your monthly debt burden is significantly higher.

What This Difference Really Means

By structuring the deal with seller financing:

- Your monthly payments are about **$1,650 lower**
- That's nearly **$20,000 per year**
- And almost **$100,000 over the first five years**

That extra cash flow isn't just comfort.
It's margin.
It's protection.
It's the ability to survive the learning curve of ownership.

In the early years, cash flow is not a bonus.
It's oxygen.

What Happens After Five Years?

This is where deal structure becomes strategy.

After five years of payments on your SBA loan:

- You will have paid down about **$265,000** of the original $700,000 loan
- Your remaining SBA balance will be about **$435,000**
- The seller note of $200,000 is still outstanding

At that point, you can refinance both together:

New loan amount:
Approximately **$635,000 total** which is less than your original SBA loan so even if your business hasn't grown you should have no problem refinancing the business

Compare that to the buyer who financed the full $900,000 from the beginning.

Even though you started with a seller-financed note, you are in a far stronger position five years later:

- lower total debt
- more equity
- a proven operating history
- and far better refinancing options

This is how structure creates future freedom.

Why Seller Financing Is So Powerful

Seller financing isn't just about needing less cash up front. It's about shaping the risk of the deal.

Because what ends most businesses isn't a lack of intelligence — it's a lack of breathing room.

Seller financing:

- lowers your early debt burden
- protects cash flow when mistakes are most likely
- aligns the seller's success with yours
- and increases your odds of staying in the game

This isn't financial trickery.
It's thoughtful design.

The Bigger Lesson

Two buyers can purchase the same business for the same price and live very different realities.

Not because one is smarter —
but because one structured the deal to protect cash flow.

That's the skill you're learning here:

How to buy freedom without suffocating it under debt.

Why Would a Seller Agree to This?

At first, you might wonder, *Why would a seller accept a deal where they don't get all their money upfront?* But there are actually **some big incentives** for them to agree:

- **Tax Benefits:** If they take all the sale proceeds at once, they could face a massive tax bill. **By spreading out their payments over time, they can defer taxes**, reducing their overall liability.
- **Guaranteed Income Stream:** Many sellers aren't looking to retire with a giant lump sum—they'd prefer a **steady, reliable income** for the next several years. Seller financing creates that for them.
- **Easier & Faster Sale:** Buyers often struggle to secure full financing from a bank. By **carrying a portion of the financing themselves**, sellers **expand the pool of**

potential buyers—increasing the chances of selling faster and at a better price.

- **Confidence in a Smooth Transition:** Many sellers care about their business's **legacy** and want to see it continue to succeed. Offering seller financing means they have a vested interest in ensuring you do well—often leading them to **help with the transition** and provide mentorship.

Can the Seller Finance the Whole Deal?

In some cases, you might find a seller who is willing to **finance 100% of the purchase price**. This is **rare**, but it does happen—especially if the business has had trouble selling, or if the owner strongly believes in you as a buyer.

However, fully seller-financed deals come with **trade-offs**:

- **You lose the bank as a second layer of vetting.** Banks don't approve loans unless they're convinced the business has solid financials. If no bank is involved, you don't get that built-in sanity check.
- **Less negotiating power.** When the seller is carrying the whole loan, they **hold all the leverage**—which often means less flexibility on price or terms.
- **Higher risk.** If the seller is eager to finance the whole deal, ask yourself why. A strong, stable business is more likely to get bank financing. If no bank will touch it, dig deeper.

That said, if structured properly, a full seller-financed deal can be a great way to acquire a business without a traditional loan. Just be extra diligent in your due diligence.

But What About Those "No Money Down" Gurus on the Internet?

By now, you've probably seen those influencers on social media claiming you can **buy a business with no money down.**

Has it happened? Yes.

Is it common? No.

And **is it usually a good idea? Also no.**

Here's the reality:

- **Most true "no money down" deals involve distressed businesses.** If a business is rock solid, why would the seller give it away for nothing?
- **Banks don't love no-money-down deals.** If you don't have any skin in the game, the risk skyrockets.
- **The sellers who offer these deals often have little choice.** If you're getting a business with no cash upfront, it's often because no one else wants it.

And have you noticed that these "gurus" are always selling you a **course** to show you how to do it?

Instead of chasing a unicorn, focus on **buying a business that will let you sleep at night and grow your financial security. A solid,**

stable business with reasonable seller financing is a far better strategy than a Hail Mary zero-down deal that could leave you buried in problems from day one.

Final Thought: This Is a Win-Win Strategy

Getting the seller to help finance your purchase isn't just about making it easier for you—it's also a smart strategy for them. With **tax advantages, steady income, and confidence that their business will continue thriving**, many sellers are open to structuring deals this way—*if you ask*.

The key? **Negotiate strategically and position it as a win-win.** Instead of focusing on how it benefits *you*, highlight how it makes the sale faster, easier, and financially smarter for them.

This is one of the most powerful tools in a business buyer's arsenal. If you use it wisely, you can own a business with less upfront risk, better cash flow, and time to learn and grow—without drowning in debt from day one.

Making Your Money Work Smarter

Buying a million-dollar home may seem like a symbol of success, but in reality, it's a personal expense that doesn't generate income and relies on your own income to pay for it. A million-dollar business, on the other hand, is a cash-flowing asset that can pay for itself, grow in value, and provide significant returns on a much smaller investment. When you buy a business, you're not just buying an asset; you're buying a source of income and a potential pathway to financial independence.

Using leverage isn't just about taking on debt; it's about using other people's money (the banks and/or the seller's) to gain control of an asset that can grow and create more wealth for you. The bank's backing and the business's cash flow give you a way to build wealth beyond what a traditional salary or home ownership could offer. By understanding how leverage works, you can take a big step toward financial freedom.

In the next chapter, we'll explore how to evaluate a business for purchase, including what financials to look for and how to assess its growth potential. Remember, buying a business isn't about having a million dollars; it's about knowing how to make your money work smarter, not harder.

Next Steps

Now that you've seen that buying a business might actually be possible, it's time to examine how to measure specific opportunities. In the next chapter, we'll explore critical financial metrics like **ROI, Cap Rate, and EBITDA**—the tools that help you determine whether a particular business, property, or investment justifies the risk for the reward you seek. By mastering these metrics, you'll be better equipped to navigate the complex balance of risk, reward, safety, and freedom in any venture you pursue.

CHAPTER 13

Finding the Right Opportunity: Demystifying Buying Math

Two Doors, Two Lives

Imagine standing in front of two open doors.

Behind one is a cozy little bakery that smells like cinnamon and possibility — early mornings, creative freedom, and the pride of watching customers linger over pastries you helped make.

Behind the other is a tidy laundromat that hums quietly through the day — steady quarters dropping into machines, predictable income, almost no surprises.

Both doors lead to "business ownership," but the lives behind them look very different. One might give you energy; the other might give you peace. One might make more money on paper; the other might give you back something rarer — *time*.

When you buy a business, you're not just buying income.

You're buying a rhythm of life.

Of course, it's not just about how those two lives feel — it's about what they can fund.

The beauty of buying a business is that numbers and lifestyle meet in the same equation. Understanding how to read those numbers is what helps you tell the difference between a business that looks good and one that truly builds freedom.

So before we go shopping, let's get comfortable with a few key concepts — starting with one you'll see everywhere: EBITDA.

Understanding EBITDA: The Business's True Earning Power

EBITDA stands for **Earnings Before Interest, Taxes, Depreciation, and Amortization** — a mouthful that really means:

"How much money does this business actually make before the accountant gets creative?"

It strips away financing, tax strategy, and paper-only expenses so you can see how strong the business is at its core.

Formula:

EBITDA = Revenue – Operating Expenses (excluding interest, taxes, depreciation, and amortization)

Example:

- Loan interest: $50,000
- Depreciation: $20,000

- Revenue: $500,000
- Operating Expenses: $350,000
- **EBITDA = $220,000**

That $220,000 is the business's *true earning power.* It's how much cash the business produces before financing or taxes — the cleanest measure of operational performance.

SDE: What You Actually Take Home

EBITDA shows how the business performs.

SDE — Seller's Discretionary Earnings — shows how much you, the owner, can live on.

Formula:

SDE = EBITDA + Owner's Salary + Perks + One-Time Expenses

It adds back personal or one-time expenses the seller chose to run through the business.

If in the example above the owner, paid herself $30,000, leased a car $20,000, and paid $10,000 for a one-time legal review, those are added back so her SDE is actually $280,000.

EBITDA = the business's strength.

SDE = the owner's lifestyle potential.

A Quick Reality Check: What You Really Keep

Brokers love to say:

"This business makes $200,000 a year!"

But SDE doesn't subtract what you'll owe on your loan.

Example:

- SDE: $200,000
- Loan Payments: $75,000
- **Actual Cash Flow: $125,000**

That $125,000 is your *Freedom Baseline* — the money that determines whether your life actually works.

It's like real estate: if your tenants pay $5,000 but the mortgage is $3,000, your *cash flow* is $2,000 — not five.

Case Study: Sarah's Sweet Treats Bakery

Sample Profit & Loss (P&L) Statement

Revenue & Expenses	Amount
Revenue (Total Sales)	**$600,000**
Cost of Goods Sold (COGS)	−$200,000
Gross Profit	**$400,000**
Operating Expenses:	
Rent	−$50,000
Utilities & Insurance	−$10,000
Payroll (Employees)	−$150,000
Marketing & Advertising	−$20,000
Supplies & Miscellaneous	−$15,000
Total Operating Expenses	**−$245,000**
EBITDA (before interest, taxes, depreciation, amortization)	**$155,000**
Loan Interest	−$15,000
Depreciation (Equipment)	−$10,000
Taxes	−$20,000
Net Operating Income (NOI)	**$110,000**

Formula Recap:

EBITDA = Revenue – Operating Expenses

→ 600,000 – 245,000 = $155,000

Why It Matters:

EBITDA shows what the bakery *really earns from operations.*

It tells you what's left once the flour settles — before financing or taxes.

How It's Used:

Buyers and investors use EBITDA to compare businesses on an even playing field.

Normalizing for Your Reality

SDE is just a snapshot of how *that* owner ran *that* business.

Maybe Sarah only worked part-time and hired extra help. If you plan to work full-time, payroll drops — SDE rises.

Or maybe she underpaid herself — your SDE falls once you pay a fair wage.

Numbers describe *her* life, not yours.

You need to **groom the numbers** for your own rhythm — your time, your systems, your boundaries.

When EBITDA and SDE Diverge

Small businesses are personal, so SDE and EBITDA often drift apart.

They're priced on **multiples of SDE** — typically 2×–4×, depending on industry and stability.

But beware of "creative" add-backs:

- A $10,000 roof repair may be "one-time," but every year something breaks.
- Legal fees or upgrades might not repeat annually, but *repairs rotate their disguise.*

If you believe every add-back, you risk overpaying for the illusion of smooth sailing.

Cap Rates: Seeing the Relationship Between Risk and Reward

Formula:

Cap Rate = (EBITDA ÷ Purchase Price) × 100

Cap Rate shows how much return you'd earn if you bought the business in cash — your yield before debt.

It's how investors compare opportunities: higher Cap Rate = higher return *and* higher risk.

Rule of Thumb	Meaning
High Cap Rate	Higher potential return — and more volatility
Low Cap Rate	Lower return — but greater stability

Your job isn't to chase the highest return.

It's to find the balance of reward and risk that fits your *life design.*

Example: Bakery vs. Laundromat

Business	Purchase Price	EBITDA	Loan Payment	Cap Rate	After-Debt Cash Flow
Sarah's Sweet Treats (Bakery)	$500,000	$155,000	$60,000	31%	$95,000
The Wash House (Laundromat)	$800,000	$100,000	$95,000	**12.5%**	**$5,000**

The bakery offers higher return — and higher personal involvement.

The laundromat offers stability — and less upside.

Different doors, different kinds of freedom.

Different Industries, Different Cap Rates

Cap Rates vary by industry:

Industry	Typical Cap Rate	Notes
Hotels	10–12%	Seasonal and labor-intensive
RV Parks	8–10%	Moderate risk, steady demand
Office Buildings	6–8%	Stable but sensitive to market shifts

For small businesses, the same logic applies:
A retail shop at 20% Cap may be owner-heavy.
A service firm at 10% may offer peace of mind.

There's no "right" Cap Rate — just the right *fit* for your goals.

What's the most useful about Cap Rates is as a quick flag regarding pricing. If the Cap rate is lower than the norm for that industry then it's potentially over priced. If it's much higher it could be a deal or could be an indication of some inherent risk or problems with the business.

Cap Rates and Interest Rates: The 3-Point Rule

When financing, the Cap Rate must stay above the loan's interest rate for positive cash flow.

Ideally, the **Cap Rate is 3 points higher** than your loan rate.

Example:

Business: $100,000 EBITDA

Loan: 80% financed, 10 years @ 6% interest

Scenario 1 — 10% Cap Rate (Healthy Spread)

- Purchase Price: $1,000,000
- Loan: $800,000
- Annual Debt: ≈ $57,600
- **Free Cash Flow: $42,400**

A 10% Cap vs. 6% interest leaves breathing room for taxes and surprises.

Scenario 2 — 6% Cap Rate (No Spread)

- Purchase Price: $1,666,000
- Loan: $1,333,000
- Annual Debt: ≈ $96,000
- **Free Cash Flow: $4,000**

Same business. Same loan rate.

But now, almost no margin. You take the risk, the bank gets the return.

A 9–10% Cap isn't greed — it's *safety*.

ROI: Measuring Your Return on Freedom

ROI (Return on Investment) is calculated as:

ROI = (Net Profit ÷ Cash Invested) × 100

This is an important number to consider. After all if a high yield secure savings account earns 5% risking your capital in a small business should yield a much better return. Otherwise, why bother.

The ROI calculation illustrates very clearly why using debt can be so powerful. It's an ROI booster. It also explains why I don't love investing in the stock market. The example below will show you why:

The Power of Leverage

Investment	Cash Invested	Annual Profit	ROI
Stock Portfolio	$150,000 (all cash)	$15,000	10%
Small Business	$150,000 purchase	$15,000	
	(20% down = $30,000)	(after debt) **50%**	

Same profit, different capital requirements.

Leverage multiplies your return but let 's not kid ourselves it also increases your risk

Only use it to amplify your freedom if it won't increase your anxiety.

Beyond the Math: The Intangibles

Numbers are important but in a small business, return on investment is never just financial.

Remember small businesses pay you twice:

- **once for your labor** — what it would cost to replace you
- **and once for your capital** — the risk you took investing your money. This is what ROI measures.

You want both returns to be worth it.

Because if a business only pays you for your time,
you haven't bought freedom —
you've just bought yourself another job.

And if it pays you financially but consumes your energy,
you haven't built wealth —
you've built a trap.

The ROI formula makes sure that the money you invested is actually making a healthy return.

However, especially for working moms the financial ROI calculation isn't enough. True ROI lives at the intersection of **money** *and* **meaning**.

At the beginning of this chapter, we looked at two businesses.

The laundromat didn't make as much.
The bakery did.

On paper, the bakery looked like the better investment.

But numbers alone don't tell the whole story.

The bakery might feed your creativity and your instinct for community but also consume you seven days a week. The laundromat might not make enough to let you quit your job but it might quietly fund your writing, your travels, or a better school for your children.

The math matters.
It always does.

But while the number part of the ROI is a calculation, *the intangible ROI is the compass.*

Because freedom doesn't live in a spreadsheet.
It lives in the margin between income and identity.

It lives in questions like:

- Who do I become inside this business? Does this business support my life, or swallow it?
- Does it expand my choices, or quietly shrink them?
- Does it give me margin — or constant pressure?
- What kind of days will I be living?
- What will this work make possible — and what will it quietly take away?

A business can be profitable and still be wrong for your life. And a business can be simpler, quieter, and less impressive — yet perfectly aligned with who you are becoming.

Because the true business you are building
is not just a company.

It is the space between your work and yourself.
Between earning and belonging.
Between survival and freedom.

And when the math and the meaning point in the same direction,
that's not just a good investment.

That's a life that fits.

Key Takeaways

1. **EBITDA** shows how profitable a business is before costs like interest and taxes — it's the clearest view of the business's true earning power.

2. **SDE** reveals how much you, as the owner, can expect to make after most expenses but *before* debt service. Remember, this number can vary based on how you choose to run the business.

3. **Cap Rate** ties the business's EBITDA to its purchase price, helping you compare returns across different opportunities — apples to apples.

4. **Risk and Growth Potential** matter as much as the raw numbers. A higher Cap Rate can mean greater upside *and* higher volatility, while a lower Cap Rate often offers more stability but less reward.

By combining these financial metrics with your personal risk tolerance and lifestyle goals, you'll make smarter, more confident choices about which opportunity — if any — is truly right for you.

And if all this math has made your eyes cross, don't worry. Once you start looking at real businesses, you'll begin to see patterns — how numbers reveal personality, potential, and sometimes even red flags. Over time, you'll learn that numbers aren't just math; they tell a story about how a business breathes and what kind of life it might create for you.

In the next chapter, we'll step beyond the spreadsheets and into the inner work of business ownership — the mindset, identity, and emotional readiness it takes to build not just a business, but a life of freedom on your own terms.

Exercise: Scouting Real Opportunities

Now for some real fun. The best way to start getting comfortable with these concepts is to start looking at real businesses for sale. Whether you're daydreaming about a coffee shop in your favorite neighborhood or an RV park near a scenic national park, exploring real opportunities will help you apply the financial tools we're about to cover.

Websites like **BizBuySell**, **LoopNet**, and **Crexi** are treasure troves of businesses and properties for sale. Think of it as window shopping, but for your financial future. The goal isn't to buy something today—it's to start seeing how businesses are valued and comparing them through the lens of EBITDA, SDE, and Cap Rates.

Let's dive in and learn how to use these tools to analyze opportunities like a pro.

Step 1: Visit Online Marketplaces

Start by visiting one or more of the following websites to explore businesses for sale:

- **BizBuySell**: Great for small businesses in various industries.
- **LoopNet**: Ideal for commercial real estate and income-producing properties.
- **Crexi**: Offers a mix of businesses and commercial real estate.

Search for businesses in areas or industries that interest you. For example:

- A local café or retail shop
- A property management company
- A service-based business like cleaning or landscaping
- Commercial properties like RV parks or storage facilities

Step 2: Collect Information

Pick three businesses or properties that catch your eye and note the following details:

1. **Asking Price**
2. **Revenue**
   - **EBITDA**
3. **Industry Type**

Step 3: Calculate the Cap Rate

Remember the formula from before and calculate the Cap Rate for each business:

Cap Rate = (EBITDA / Purchase Price) × 100

Write down the Cap Rate for each business. Which one offers the highest return? Does the higher Cap Rate align with the level of risk you're comfortable with?

Step 4: Compare Industries

Look at the type of business or property and consider the average Cap Rates for that industry:

- **Retail or restaurants**: Typically, higher Cap Rates due to volatility.
- **RV parks or storage units**: Moderate Cap Rates with steady demand.
- **Office buildings or professional services**: Lower Cap Rates with long-term stability.

How do the Cap Rates you calculated compare to industry norms? Are the businesses priced fairly, or does something seem off?

Step 5: Reflect on Control and Risk

Think about how much control you would have in running each business:

- Would you need specialized knowledge or skills to succeed?
- How stable does the income look?

- What external factors could impact the business, such as seasonality or economic changes?

Write down which opportunity feels the most aligned with your skills, goals, and risk tolerance.

Optional Bonus: Play with Financing

For one of the businesses you selected, assume you're financing the purchase with a 20% down payment and an 8% interest loan. Calculate:

- **Loan Amount**: 80% of the purchase price.
- **Debt Service**: Use an online SBA loan calculator to estimate annual payments.
- **Free Cash Flow**: Subtract the debt service from the EBITDA

Does the free cash flow provide enough breathing room to cover unexpected expenses and still generate a return?

Goal of the Exercise

This exercise isn't about making an actual purchase—it's about building your confidence in analyzing opportunities. The more you practice, the easier it will become to spot the right deal when the time comes. So have fun exploring, and don't be afraid to dream big!

CHAPTER 14

The Inner and Outer Work of Building a Business

From Strategy to Self-Mastery

We've been on quite a journey together. If you've made it this far, I hope you're feeling inspired and confident about the changes you want to make in your life. You've learned why a seat at the table isn't enough, how to shift your mindset, how to evaluate risk and reward, and how to see the possibility of starting or buying a business that truly works for you.

But now comes the hard part—actually doing it.

Ideas and strategies are valuable, but without execution, they're just words on a page. And execution? That starts in your mind.

You can have the best business plan, the strongest financial strategy, and a clear roadmap to success, but if the stories you tell yourself about money, work, and worth are holding you back, you'll stay stuck.

Before we put these principles into action, we need to address the *internal* work.

The Stories We Inherit

Most of us don't reach adulthood with a neutral relationship to money. Our financial beliefs were formed long before we ever earned a dollar.

From childhood, we absorb messages about money, work, and risk—messages that shape our self-perception and influence every financial decision we make.

Some come from family dynamics —the way our parents handled (or didn't handle) money. Others come from cultural expectations, gender norms, or economic circumstances.

Common money messages you may have heard growing up:

- "Money doesn't grow on trees."
- "Rich people are greedy."
- "Security comes from a steady paycheck."
- "Investing is complicated—you'll lose your money."
- "It's not polite to talk about money."

Messages often directed specifically at women:

- "Find a stable job with benefits."
- "Don't take big risks—you have a family to think about."
- "A man who is good with money is a good catch."
- "Women aren't as good at math or finance."

Even women raised in financially secure homes are rarely taught how to *build* wealth. We're taught to budget, save, and be responsible. Men are encouraged to take risks; women are encouraged to seek stability.

The result?

Many women feel deeply uncomfortable with the idea of financial independence outside of employment. We internalize the belief that success means getting a "good job," staying out of debt, and making safe choices.

But here's the truth:

- Playing it safe can be the riskiest thing you do.
- Financial freedom doesn't come from working harder—it comes from working smarter.
- The rules you were taught aren't the only rules.

If you've ever felt resistance to starting a business, investing, or leaving a "safe" job, ask yourself:

What's the story I've been told about money—and is it actually true?

Rewriting the Narrative: From Limitation to Possibility

Once you recognize the stories that have shaped your beliefs, you have a choice:

- Continue believing them.
- Or rewrite them.

Many of us assume our financial mindset is fixed—as if our view of money and risk is simply part of who we are. But these beliefs are *learned*, which means they can be *unlearned.*

Let's flip some common limiting beliefs:

Old Belief	New Narrative
"I'm not good with money."	"I may not have been taught financial skills, but I can learn them now."
"Starting a business is too risky."	"Relying on one job for all my income is risky. Owning an asset creates security."
"I don't have what it takes to be an entrepreneur."	"Entrepreneurship isn't a personality type—it's a skill set I can develop."

Recognizing your internal scripts is the first step. Rewriting them takes practice. It's not enough to understand the new idea—you have to start *acting* as if you believe it.

Try this:

- If you've always been afraid of investing, learn about one type of investment that interests you.
- If you've felt you're not "business-minded," surround yourself with people who are.
- If financial decisions feel overwhelming, start small—make one confident choice today.

But here's where it gets tricky: even when we consciously work to change our beliefs, there are deeper forces at play.

That's because our money stories aren't just ideas—they're tied to our *identities*.

And those identities are shaped by something even more fundamental: our **money archetypes.**

Your Inner Team: The Three Key Archetypes

You've learned how money stories shape your choices. But beneath those stories lives something deeper—the inner cast of characters that runs your financial life. Every decision you make—whether to spend, save, invest, or start something new—isn't made by a single "you." It's made by the different parts of you that carry old experiences, talents, and fears.

These parts form your inner team—and learning how to align them is the key to creating a business that reflects your whole self. The challenge is that, for many of us, these archetypes operate beneath the surface. By bringing them into awareness, we can harness the powerful ones, calm the problematic ones, and ensure they work together—so you move forward with clarity instead of chaos.

Just as every successful business depends on strong leadership and a balanced team, your financial success depends on understanding the roles within yourself. The following money archetypes—based on the work of money coach Deborah Price—offer a framework for recognizing which parts of you are leading the way and which may need a little guidance.

Magician – The Visionary

This is the part of you that sees opportunities others miss. The Magician creates ideas, imagines possibilities, and connects dots in unexpected ways. Every business starts with an idea, and your Magician is the one whispering, *"What if...?"*

When your Magician is strong: You're innovative, able to see future trends, and can generate big, exciting possibilities. You're also open and aware of synchronicities, uncanny timing and moments of unscripted luck.

When your Magician is weak: You may struggle to trust yourself, dismiss good ideas too quickly, or feel paralyzed by doubt.

The Creator/Artist – The Skilled Expert

The Creator/Artist taps into your **talents, skills, and craftsmanship**. It's the part of you that can take the Magician's vision and say, *"I know how to make this real."* Whether it's crafting a product, developing a service, or leveraging your natural abilities, your Creator/Artist is the key to **producing value**.

When your Creator/Artist is strong: You're deeply connected to your skills, take pride in your work, and find **fulfillment in creating**.

When your Creator/Artist is weak: You might feel like an **imposter**, doubt your abilities, or struggle to see your own worth.

The Warrior – The Execution Machine

The Warrior **gets things done.** This is the part of you that moves forward, takes action, and follows through. You can have the greatest idea in the world, but without the Warrior's energy, nothing happens.

When your Warrior is strong: You take decisive action, follow through, and don't let fear stop you.

When your Warrior is weak: You may **procrastinate**, feel stuck in endless planning, or avoid taking risks.

Are Your Archetypes in Balance?

When these **three archetypes work together**, you have a powerful **inner team** driving your success:

- The **Magician** sparks ideas.
- The **Creator/Artist** brings talent and skills to make those ideas real.
- The **Warrior** takes action and gets things done.

If one of these is **out of balance**, it can **slow you down**. Maybe you're full of **ideas** but never execute (too much Magician, not enough Warrior). Or maybe you're **a perfectionist** with your work but afraid to take it to market (Creator/Artist dominating, Warrior missing).

The Archetypes We Want to Transform

While the **Magician, Creator, and Warrior** help us succeed, we also have archetypes that can hold us back. These are **formed in childhood** based on the money behaviors we saw in our families.

The Innocent – The Avoider

The Innocent avoids dealing with money—either out of fear, lack of confidence, or a belief that someone else will always handle it. This archetype may ignore financial realities, avoid looking at bank statements, or assume that "everything will just work out." They often rely on a partner, employer, or even the universe to provide, rather than actively managing their own financial future.

When the Innocent is active: You may feel intimidated by financial discussions, procrastinate on money decisions, or feel overwhelmed by anything more complex than a paycheck.

The Transformation: The Innocent must step into financial awareness. This doesn't mean becoming an expert overnight, but rather developing **basic financial literacy** and shifting from avoidance to empowerment. Small steps—like tracking expenses or scheduling a money check-in—build confidence.

Ask yourself: What's one small financial task I can tackle today that I've been avoiding?

The Fool – The Thrill-Seeker

The Fool loves the **excitement** of money—whether it's chasing get-rich-quick schemes, making impulsive purchases, or investing in things they don't fully understand. They're optimistic and bold, which can be a strength, but they often lack patience and discipline.

When the Fool is active: You might **jump into investments or businesses** without doing enough due diligence. You might spend money as soon as you get it or constantly chase the next big thing without a real plan.

The Transformation: The Fool doesn't need to stop being bold, but they do need **a strategy**. Learning to balance **calculated risk** with **thoughtful planning** allows them to use their adventurous spirit wisely. The Fool benefits from **trusted advisors** who can offer perspective before they leap into decisions.

Ask yourself: Am I making this financial decision based on **a plan**—or am I just chasing a quick win?

The Martyr – The Self-Sacrificer

The Martyr prioritizes everyone else's needs before their own, often **at the expense of their financial security**. They may support adult children, lend money they can't afford to lose, undercharge for their work, or refuse to invest in themselves because it feels "selfish."

When the Martyr is active: You might feel **guilt** around charging fair prices, hesitate to say no when someone asks for financial help, or believe that financial success comes at the cost of relationships.

The Transformation: The Martyr must shift from **self-sacrifice to self-worth**—realizing that financial stability allows them to take care of others **without depleting themselves**. Learning to set boundaries and prioritize their own future is **not selfish—it's essential**.

Ask yourself: If I were advising my best friend, what would I tell them about their financial needs? Now, can I apply that same kindness to myself?

The good news? These archetypes can be transformed. Awareness is the first step.

- → If you recognize yourself in any of these, it's time to shift the narrative.

- → One of the best ways to start? **Take the free Money Type Quiz** at **www.phinevo.com..**

This quiz will help you see **which money patterns are running in the background of your life**—and how to shift them to support your success.

If you find that your **inner team** is struggling in certain areas, that's okay. The good news is, you don't have to do this alone. That's where your **external team** comes in.

The Archetypes in Action: Sarah's Story

To understand how these archetypes shape our financial reality—and how we can shift them—let's look at Sarah's story.

Sarah grew up in a family where money was always tight. Her parents, both hard-working but financially stressed, often argued about bills, and the phrase "We can't afford that" was a constant refrain in her childhood.

She internalized two powerful but contradictory money beliefs:

- From her mother, who handled the budget with exhaustion and sacrifice, she absorbed the Martyr archetype. Money was something you worked endlessly for, but never quite had enough of. Stability came from scraping by and playing it safe.
- From her father, who dreamed of "making it big" but was always chasing the next get-rich-quick scheme, she inherited the Fool archetype. She learned that financial freedom seemed just out of reach—if only the "next big thing" worked out.

As an adult, these beliefs clashed. Sarah was afraid to take risks with money, fearing instability like her mother. But she also carried the deep-seated belief that "real wealth" came from some big break, not steady progress.

She felt trapped—working long hours in a stable (but low-paying) job, afraid to invest, yet resentful that financial freedom seemed reserved for other people.

Shifting the Narrative

Sarah's transformation began with a simple realization: **the patterns she inherited were not her destiny.**

She started small.

- ☑ **Step 1: Awareness** – She took the **free Money Type Quiz** on my website and recognized how her Martyr and Fool archetypes were keeping her stuck.

- ☑ **Step 2: Reframing Risk** – Instead of seeing investing as dangerous, she reframed it as a way to create stability. She started setting aside just $50 a month into a low-risk index fund—something her Martyr could accept as "responsible" while still allowing her Fool to feel like she was working toward a bigger vision.

- ☑ **Step 3: Building an Inner Team** – She strengthened her Warrior archetype by making financial learning a habit. She read books about women and wealth, listened to podcasts, and **joined a mastermind group** of other women looking to break free from financial fear.

- ☑ **Step 4: Taking Control** – She finally left her stagnant job and used her savings to buy a small business—a mobile pet grooming service—where she could set her own hours and own an income-generating asset rather than just trading time for money.

The Outcome

Sarah didn't transform overnight. She still felt fear when making big decisions. But she kept taking action.

Today, she's not only financially stable, but growing. Her business is thriving, and she's on track to buy a second mobile grooming van next year. She no longer waits for a big break or plays it safe out of fear—she actively builds wealth on her own terms.

And the best part?

Sarah's kids don't hear "We can't afford that" as a default answer. Instead, they hear, "Let's figure out how to make it happen."

Your External Team: You Can't Do This Alone—And You Shouldn't

Your Inner Team—your mindset, your beliefs, and your personal strengths—is the foundation for success. But even the strongest mindset can't replace expertise, experience, and the support of people who know the terrain.

At this point, you've done the inner work. Now, it's time to build your Outer Team—the people who will help you turn this vision into reality.

A business deal isn't just about numbers on a spreadsheet—it's about real people, real money, and real stakes. Emotions can cloud judgment. Sellers can be persuasive. Unexpected obstacles will show up. And the truth is, even the most experienced business buyers don't do this alone.

That's why the people you surround yourself with—your Inner and Outer Team—matter just as much as the business itself.

The smartest investors, entrepreneurs, and dealmakers all have one thing in common: **they know how to assemble a team that makes them stronger.**

Maybe you don't know how to analyze financial statements like a pro—but your accountant does.

Maybe you're not sure how to structure the legal terms of your deal—but your attorney does.

Maybe you've never raised capital before—but your banker does.

You don't have to become a financial analyst, a legal expert, or a deal-structuring genius overnight. But you **do** need to know who to trust, what questions to ask, and how to build a team that protects your interests.

The best business owners don't just manage businesses—they manage relationships.

Whether it's your mentors, advisors, legal and financial professionals, or even a business-savvy friend who helps you think clearly when emotions run high—having the right people in your corner can be the difference between success and regret.

Who You Need in Your Corner

Now that we've covered why having the right team is essential, let's talk about exactly who should be in your corner...

1. A Business Owner's Mastermind Group

You need a circle of like-minded business owners—people who understand the journey you're on and can offer guidance, support, and accountability.

- A mastermind group helps problem-solve challenges,
- Shares lessons learned from real-world experience, and
- Keeps you motivated when self-doubt creeps in.

Tip: If you don't have a mastermind group, look for local entrepreneur meetups, online communities, or small business groups. The best advice often comes from people just a few steps ahead of you.

2. A Great Commercial Business Broker

If you're buying a business, a skilled business broker is invaluable. They help you find solid businesses for sale, negotiate deals, and navigate the buying process.

What to look for in a broker:

- ✅ **Experience** in selling businesses in your industry.
- ✅ A strong track record of **successful deals.**
- ✅ Transparency and a **genuine interest in helping buyers succeed.**

3. A Lawyer and a CPA (Your Due Diligence Team)

When buying a business, you need a sharp legal and financial team to make sure you don't step into a financial minefield.

- A **business attorney** ensures contracts, leases, and agreements protect you.
- A **CPA (Certified Public Accountant)** reviews financials, tax history, and liabilities so there are no hidden surprises.

Tip: Don't just use **any** lawyer or CPA—work with professionals experienced in business transactions.

4. A Bank Loan Officer Who Believes in You

If you're using **an SBA loan** or other financing to buy a business, your banker is your partner. A good loan officer will:

- Help you understand loan options and requirements
- Make sure you get the best financing terms possible
- Provide insights into what lenders look for

Tip: Develop a relationship with a lender early—even before you need funding. This will give you an edge when it's time to secure financing.

5. Your State's Small Business Resources

If you live in the United States, you have access to *free* small business resources that many aspiring entrepreneurs don't even realize exist. Every state has organizations dedicated to helping small business owners and entrepreneurs—offering free coaching, mentorship, and educational resources.

Here are a few key places to start:

- **Small Business Development Centers (SBDCs)** – Funded by the **SBA (Small Business Administration)**, these centers provide **free** business coaching, classes on business planning and finance, and guidance on everything from marketing to securing funding. You can find your local SBDC at **www.sba.gov/local-assistance/sbdc**.
- **SCORE (Service Corps of Retired Executives)** – A nonprofit organization that offers *free* one-on-one mentoring from **seasoned business owners and executives.** You can connect with a SCORE mentor at **www.score.org**.
- **Women's Business Centers (WBCs)** – If you're a woman entrepreneur, WBCs provide targeted support, coaching, and networking opportunities. Find one near you at **www.sba.gov/local-assistance/wbc**.
- **State-Specific Entrepreneur Programs** – Many state governments have their own entrepreneurial support programs, offering everything from grants and incubator programs to legal and financial guidance. A quick search for "**[Your State] Small Business Assistance**" can lead you to additional resources in your area.

These programs exist to help you succeed—so take advantage of them! Whether you need help writing a business plan, securing funding, or just getting clarity on your next step, there are free experts available to guide you.

If you live outside of the United States use the same key words above to find free support resources for your country or province.

Final Thought: You Don't Have to Do This Alone

Building a successful business isn't just about what you know—it's about who you surround yourself with. When you align your inner team and assemble the right external team, you set yourself up for confidence, resilience, and long-term success.

The road ahead won't always be easy—but with the right people in your corner, you'll be able to navigate every challenge with clarity and strength.

Now, it's time to take action.

You've done the thinking, the planning, and the learning.

The next step is making it real. And with the right team?

You've got this.

Exercise: What is my Money Story?

Take a moment to reflect on your own relationship with money.

- What were the messages you absorbed about money growing up?
- Do you tend to play it safe financially, or do you take big risks without fully thinking them through?

- Do you feel confident making financial decisions, or do you defer to others?

Understanding your dominant archetypes—the strengths you naturally lean on and the patterns that may be holding you back—gives you insight into where to focus your growth.

The next step? Learning to put these strengths into action. Because knowing your patterns is important, but what you do next is what truly changes your future.

CHAPTER 15

Buying Right: How to Structure and Negotiate a Smart Deal

Now that you have the right people in place, you're ready for the final, crucial step—negotiating a deal that truly works for you.

This is where everything comes together: the right business, the right team, and the right terms. Buying a business is one of the biggest financial decisions you'll ever make. It's not just about finding the right opportunity—it's about buying it the right way.

A great deal isn't just about the business itself; it's about **how** you structure the purchase, **what** terms you negotiate, and **how much** risk you take on.

You can take an average business and create a great deal—or buy an amazing business and ruin it with bad terms.

Step 1 | Evaluate the Business Beyond the Surface

A strong business isn't defined only by revenue or industry. What matters most is predictable, sustainable cash flow—and how easily you can step into ownership.

Key questions to ask:

1. **Is the business priced on real numbers or "future potential"?**
   Never pay for projections; pay for verified past performance.

2. **Can you add value quickly without major risk?**
   Look for fixable inefficiencies—outdated marketing, weak branding, or operational gaps you can close.

3. **Does the cash flow support your financial needs after debt?**
   If it doesn't provide enough income after loan payments, it's not a good deal—no matter how much "potential" it has.

4. **Does the risk match your stress tolerance?**
   A seasonal business that earns 80 percent of its profit in two months might work for someone else, but if you need stability, it's a red flag.

Once a business checks these boxes, it's time to structure the purchase to minimize risk and maximize return.

Step 2 | Structure the Purchase to Your Advantage

Most people assume buying a business requires a huge upfront investment. In reality, smart structuring can lower your cash outlay and align incentives.

Leveraging Seller Financing

Because small businesses are often difficult to sell, many sellers are willing to finance part of the purchase price.

Why this helps you:

- Reduces upfront cash required
- Limits bank debt and personal risk
- Keeps the seller invested in your success

Example — Buying a Business for $500,000

- 40 % seller financing = $200,000 seller note
- 50 % SBA loan = $250,000
- 10 % cash down = $50,000

You've acquired a half-million-dollar business while investing only $50,000 of your own money—and the business's cash flow covers the debt.

Negotiating Strong Terms

Price isn't everything; structure often matters more.

- **Tie payments to performance.**
  If the seller predicts future growth, make part of their payout contingent on it.
- **Use seller financing as a hedge.**
  If issues surface post-sale, you're not carrying 100 percent of the risk.
- **Ensure a smooth transition.**
  Negotiate for the seller to remain involved for 3–6 months. Continuity protects both sides.

Case Study: Laura Buys a Boutique Hotel— Why Price Isn't Everything

After running a successful vacation rental business, Laura was ready to level up to a fully operational hotel. She found the perfect property—a 20-room boutique hotel in a popular tourist destination, listed at $2 million. The hotel had solid fundamentals: 75% occupancy at an average nightly rate of $150, bringing in $821,000 in annual revenue. However, the rooms were outdated, and Laura saw an opportunity to improve the business by refreshing the décor, updating the website, and optimizing pricing.

As she explored financing options, Laura realized that how she structured the deal could have a bigger impact than just negotiating the price down. Here's how her two possible deals played out:

Scenario 1 — Lower Price, Traditional SBA Financing

- Purchase price: $1.7 million
- Down payment: 20 % ($340,000)
- Loan: $1.36 million at 7.5 % (25 years)
- Monthly payment: ≈ $9,900
- Cash available for improvements: none

Laura secured a discount but tied up all her capital. With no upgrade budget, she couldn't raise rates quickly.

Pros: lower price and debt
Cons: limited growth, slower returns

Scenario 2 — Full Price with Seller Financing

- Purchase price: $2 million
- SBA loan: $1.6 million at 7.5 % (25 years)
- Seller note: $300,000 at 5 % interest-only (5 years)
- Down payment: $100,000
- Cash reserved for renovations: $240,000
- Monthly payments: $11,650 (SBA) + $1,250 (seller) = $12,900

That $240,000 war-chest allowed immediate room updates and marketing improvements. Within a year, she raised rates to $175 per night, boosting revenue to $958,000 — an extra $137,000.

Pros: fast revenue growth, higher ROI
Cons: higher total debt, but stronger overall return

Scenario	Price	Down Payment	Monthly Debt Service	Cash for Growth	Annual Net Income (after debt)	ROI on Investment	Seller Income
1 Lower Price	$1.7 M	$340 K	$9,900	$0	$187,800	55 %	—
2 Seller Financing	$2 M	$100 K	$12,900	$240 K	$248,400	248 %	$15,000 (interest)

Key Takeaways:

Scenario 2, despite the higher price, gives Laura much greater returns because she can improve the business faster and generate higher revenue.

Her ROI is 248% in Scenario 2 versus only 55% in Scenario 1—a huge difference.

The seller benefits too—earning $15,000 per year in interest over the next five years instead of just taking a price cut.

By carrying a seller note, the seller also reduces their capital gains tax burden—instead of paying a lump sum tax on the entire sale in year one, they spread out their income over five years.

Many sellers appreciate the security of continued income while transitioning into retirement or their next venture. In this case, the seller gets five years of steady payments rather than just a lump sum.

In Scenario 1, Laura is stuck with the same outdated business, unable to raise rates quickly. In Scenario 2, she buys a better-performing business and scales much faster.

Final Lesson: Price Isn't Everything—Terms Can Be the Advantage

If Laura had only focused on price, she might have thought that getting a $300K discount was the better deal. But by understanding how seller financing could give her leverage, she structured a better deal—one that increased her cash flow and maximized ROI while also benefiting the seller.

Buying a business isn't just about negotiating the lowest price—it's about buying the right deal in the right way. Sometimes, better terms can give you more control, cash flow, and freedom, setting you up for a much stronger financial future.

Step 3: Avoiding the Biggest Buying Mistakes

Buying a business is one of the most financially transformative decisions you can make—but it's also a decision you have to get right.

It's easy to fall in love with an opportunity that looks profitable on paper or excites you emotionally. Maybe the seller has a great story. Maybe the location is perfect, or you can already picture yourself running the business. But excitement alone won't guarantee success.

That's why the most dangerous mistakes buyers make aren't just about financials—they're about mindset.

Does this business align with your risk tolerance? Your strengths? Your ability to weather inevitable downturns?

And most critically: Are you paying the right price?

Overpaying—The Mistake You May Never Recover From

The #1 way to lose money on a business? **Overpaying.**

Unlike buying a house, you can't just put a business back on the market and expect a quick resale. Businesses take time to sell—often years—and finding the right buyer willing to pay your price is never guaranteed.

It's a truism in business: **you make money when you buy, not when you sell.** What that really means is that your profit is locked in the day you close the deal. If you pay too much, the first few years of ownership are spent just trying to earn back what you overpaid. You're not building wealth yet—you're digging out of a hole. A business that should have been a strong return can turn into years of break-even just because the price was too high. If the numbers don't make sense from day one, walk away.

But why do buyers overpay in the first place?

Because emotion sneaks in. Buyers fall in love with the story, the location, or the dream of being their own boss. They assume that if a business is priced at a certain number, it must be worth that much. But price and value aren't the same thing—and sellers don't always base their asking price on financial reality.

Sellers Often Have a Number in Their Head—And It's Not Always Based on Reality

Many business owners anchor to a number based on what they want for their business, not what it's actually worth. Maybe they heard a friend sold for a certain multiple, or maybe they're emotionally attached to what they built and think it's worth more than the market says.

Some sellers focus on what they need for retirement, not what the business cash flow actually justifies. Others might have invested a ton of money in renovations, technology, or branding—but that doesn't mean a buyer should pay a premium for their past decisions.

A great business at the wrong price is still a bad deal.

What Are You Really Buying - Understanding What You're Paying For: The Three Components of Business Valuation

It's hard to understand what is the right price unless you understand where a price even comes from. The purchase price is typically made up of **three key components**:

1. **Tangible Assets:** These are the physical things you can see and touch—equipment, inventory, real estate (if included), and anything else of material value. If you were buying a restaurant, for example, this would include the kitchen appliances, tables, chairs, and existing food stock. These assets have a **resale value**, meaning if the business closed tomorrow, you could sell them off.

2. **A Multiple of Net Operating Income (NOI):** Most businesses are priced based on a **multiple of the income**

they generate. The multiple varies by industry—some businesses, like manufacturing, may sell for 3–5x their annual net income, while others, like SaaS (software as a service) companies, might command much higher valuations. The more stable and predictable the income, the higher the multiple the seller can usually justify.

3   **Goodwill:** This is the **intangible** value of the business—the brand, customer loyalty, reputation, and market positioning. Unlike tangible assets, goodwill only exists if customers keep coming back. It's the reason an established coffee shop in a prime location is worth far more than a new café selling the same drinks down the street.

Goodwill is a key reason why most businesses sell for more than just the value of their physical assets—because in theory, you're not just buying equipment, you're buying the revenue stream that comes with it. But not all goodwill is created equal.

When Goodwill Doesn't Transfer—The Gluten-Free Bakery That Wasn't Worth It

Typically, goodwill stays with the business when a new owner steps in—customers remain loyal, employees continue running daily operations, and the brand's reputation holds strong. But what happens when the goodwill is tied to the owner personally?

That's exactly what I realized when evaluating a gluten-free bakery for sale.

On paper, the numbers were great. The business had strong cash flow and included valuable tangible assets—expensive commercial ovens, mixers, and top-of-the-line kitchen equipment. But I had to ask myself:

Was I buying an actual business—or just a name that wouldn't mean anything once the owner left?

The seller was a two-time winner of *Cupcake Wars*, and that notoriety had built a loyal following. Customers weren't just coming for gluten-free treats—they were coming because of *her* reputation as a celebrity baker.

The problem? She was leaving.

Even worse, she didn't want to include two of her most popular recipes in the sale.

At this point, I had to ask: What was I actually paying for?

Sure, the bakery had a great name, but would customers keep coming if the well-known owner was no longer there? Would they still drive across town if the best-selling items were no longer on the menu?

Goodwill only has value if it stays with the business—not just with the seller.

Without the owner's name and signature recipes, this wasn't the same bakery customers had fallen in love with. What I would have been left with was just another gluten-free bakery. And if that's all it was, then the price she was asking was way too high—because it was based on *her* success, not what the business could do without her.

If a business's success is too tied to the owner's personal reputation, skill, or relationships, you're not buying a transferable business.

And that's exactly why I walked away.

The Fit Factor—Just Because It's Profitable Doesn't Mean It's Right

A business might look great on paper, but if it doesn't align with your financial and emotional bandwidth, it's a bad deal for you.

Some businesses come with extreme seasonality, unpredictable cash flow, or long hours that don't fit your life. Others might require a skill set you don't have—or a level of financial risk you're not comfortable with.

This is exactly what I realized when I walked away from what seemed like a perfectly profitable business...

The Business That Looked Great—But Kept Me Up at Night

A few months into my business search, I came across what seemed like a dream deal—a home furnishings store in a charming small town. The business had been around for twenty years, had a loyal customer base, and, on paper, was a solid moneymaker. The owner was ready to retire.

After debt payments, it would put $200,000 a year in my pocket. That's a life-changing number for many people. I could already picture what I'd do with that income—invest in other ventures, put money away for my kids, maybe even take an extended trip. It checked all the financial boxes.

But as I dug into the details, and asked for the financials broken down by month instead of by year I discovered something less than ideal.

The store's sales weren't steady throughout the year. In fact, 80% of the revenue came in just two months—November and December. The rest of the year, the business just broke even or operated at a loss. It obviously made enough in those peak months to cover its lean seasons as the annual numbers showed, but those months had to go perfectly. One bad holiday season could wipe out the entire year's profits.

I pictured myself lying awake in August, staring at the ceiling, wondering if this year's holiday rush would be strong enough. What if a recession hit? What if a major online retailer slashed prices and undercut the store right before the season started? What if bad weather kept shoppers away? I'd be at the mercy of things completely out of my control, crossing my fingers that two months of sales would be enough to cover the rest of the year.

I realized something important: a "great deal" isn't just about numbers—it's about your ability to stomach the risks that come with those numbers.

For someone else, this deal might have been perfect. Maybe another buyer thrived on seasonal businesses, loved the rush of a make-or-break sales cycle, and had a high tolerance for uncertainty. But for me?

I like to sleep at night.

A business that only made money two months out of the year wasn't freedom for me—it was a gamble.

And that's the part of business buying that doesn't always show up on spreadsheets: your personal risk tolerance matters just as much as the numbers.

I walked away from the deal. Not because it was a bad business, but because it was the wrong business for me.

If you're thinking about buying a business, don't just ask whether it makes money—ask whether you can live with how it makes money. Because financial freedom isn't just about income; it's about peace of mind.

Step 4: Assess Whether You Can Step Back In If Needed

When the Business Works— But You Couldn't Step In

At one point in my search, I found what seemed like a perfectly profitable car repair business in my hometown. It was well-established, had great cash flow, and already had a team of trained mechanics on staff.

On paper, it checked all my boxes. I wasn't planning to be the one fixing cars—I knew I could handle everything else: sales, marketing, customer service, and business strategy. I had no doubt I could grow the business and increase profitability.

But as I thought through the long-term risks, a nagging feeling set in.

What if the economy took a downturn? What if I needed to cut costs? What if key employees left unexpectedly? I couldn't step in and do the work myself.

That didn't mean I had to be able to perform every role in any business I bought—but it did violate one principle that had always given me a deep sense of security:

If times got tough, I could personally step in and keep the business afloat

With my hotels, I knew I could clean rooms, check guests in, and manage reservations if needed. If cash got tight, I could cut some payroll and temporarily take on more responsibility. It wasn't ideal, but it meant I'd never feel completely at the mercy of employees, the economy, or market conditions.

But with a mechanic shop? If things got lean, there was no world in which I could step in and start fixing cars.

This was a critical realization for me, and it's something every buyer should consider:

You don't need to be the best at every job in your business. But if you don't have the technical skills to do any of the core work, you're fully dependent on other people.

That might be fine for some business owners—there are plenty of investor-owners who operate businesses they couldn't personally run. But for me, that level of dependence felt too risky.

This business negated one of the biggest hidden advantages of business ownership:

If life throws a curveball, you can always step in and take a more active role to maintain stability.

That's control you never get in a corporate job.

When you work for someone else, layoffs, restructuring, and pay cuts happen outside your control. But when you own a business, you *always* have options. You can adjust, adapt, or step back in to keep things running.

And that's real financial security.

Step 5: The Final Litmus Test—Does This Deal Give You Freedom?

At the end of the day, why are you doing this?

You're not buying a business just to own one. You're not doing this to swap one job for another. You're not chasing a title or an illusion of success.

You're doing this because you want more control over your life.

So before you sign on the dotted line, ask yourself:

*Does this deal actually give me more freedom—or just a
new kind of stress?*

A great deal isn't just about profit potential, impressive revenue numbers, or even a great price. A great deal is one that serves your life, not just your bank account.

It also has to align with your personality, your lifestyle, and what actually excites you.

Otherwise, **you're just building a cage with a better view.**

Before buying anything ask:

- ✔ Does this business replace your income without requiring constant work?
- ✔ Can it grow and build wealth over time?
- ✔ Does it give you control over your financial future?
- ✔ Does it feel like a business you'd actually enjoy running?
- ✔ Most importantly—does it let you sleep at night?

If the answer to these questions is **yes**, you're on the right path.

But if something in your gut is telling you it's not the right fit—listen.

The Business That Made Perfect Sense—But Felt Completely Wrong

I once looked at buying a specialty shoe store. On paper, it was a dream deal—a 30% cap rate (basically unheard of), strong cash flow, and a motivated seller.

But the more I thought about it, the more I realized: *I would hate every second of it.*

The idea of being stuck in a store all day, waiting for customers to trickle in, made my stomach turn. At least in my hotel, I knew when I had to be there—occupancy dictated my time. Retail, however, meant showing up every day, whether business was booming or completely dead.

And then there was the lease. Five more years tied to a location I wasn't sure I wanted to commit to. Some would see that as a perk—predictability, stability. But to me? It felt like a prison sentence.

Could I have convinced myself to buy it? Sure. The numbers made sense. It was a "smart" deal. But I've learned something over the years:

The smartest deal is the one that actually aligns with who you are.

The best career advice I never got?

How you spend your days is how you spend your life, so don't buy yourself a job you don't want.

The Biggest Mistake Isn't Overpaying—It's Not Taking Action

When I said the biggest mistake was over paying for a business, I was wrong – well sort of. After all the analysis, due diligence, and number crunching, at some point, you have to take the leap.

I included stories of deals that I walked away from because knowing when to say **NO** is extremely important. Buying the wrong business will create the opposite of the freedom and security that this book is about.

However, the worst mistake isn't buying the wrong business.

It's never buying one at all.

The truth is, *there is no perfect business.* No matter how much due diligence you do, there will always be surprises, challenges, and problems you didn't anticipate.

If you're waiting for a business that comes with zero stress, no setbacks, and a crystal-clear path forward, you'll be waiting forever.

I learned this the hard way when I bought my first hotel. As you may recall, I was pregnant with my first child when I took the leap into business ownership. I had a solid plan—until it all went sideways.

My one and only front desk employee gave me *two weeks' notice... exactly two weeks before my due date.*

I burst into tears.

Was I hormonal? Absolutely.

Was I also terrified? 100%.

This wasn't part of the plan. I wasn't supposed to be scrambling to hire someone while on the verge of giving birth. How was I going to train a new employee while recovering from labor? How was I going to keep the business running when I barely knew what I was doing myself?

For a brief moment, I thought, what have I done?

But here's the thing—this is business ownership. Things will go wrong. It's not a question of if, but *when*.

Luckily, when I told my OB-GYN what had happened (probably in the context of "Can we keep the baby in there a few more months?"), she mentioned someone she knew who was reliable and looking for work. I hired them, and the crisis was averted.

The point is, if you wait for a business where nothing ever goes wrong, you'll never buy one at all.

Every single business owner has had a "What the hell did I just do?" moment. Every business has unexpected fires to put out. But you figure it out.

Waiting for the perfect business is like waiting for the perfect moment to have a baby. It doesn't exist.

What does exist? The opportunity to build something that gives you freedom—even if it comes with a few unexpected meltdowns along the way.

Buying a business isn't about taking a reckless risk—it's about making a smart, calculated move toward freedom.

And if you buy right, structure wisely, and negotiate terms that protect your future?

You're not just buying a business.

You're buying back your life.

From Theory to Action—Making the Leap

At this point, you've learned how to identify a great business, assess risk, negotiate smartly, and structure a deal that works for you. You've seen the importance of buying at the right price, structuring terms that protect you, and choosing a business that aligns with your life—not just your bank account.

But knowing what to do and actually doing it are two different things.

A business deal isn't just about numbers on a spreadsheet—it's about real people, real money, and real stakes. Emotions can cloud judgment. Sellers can be persuasive. Unexpected obstacles will show up. And the truth is, no matter how much research you do, there will always be unknowns.

So how do you move forward with confidence?

You remember why you're doing this in the first place.

You're not buying a business just to own one. You're not making this leap because it sounds impressive or because you want a new challenge for the sake of it.

You're doing this because you want more control over your life.

And that means making bold but smart decisions.

It means trusting your instincts while leaning on the knowledge you've gained, the numbers you've analyzed, and the team you've built around you. It means knowing that while no deal is ever perfect, you are capable of handling whatever comes next.

Will it be scary? Sometimes.

Will there be moments when you question everything? Almost certainly.

But that's what growth feels like. That's what stepping into ownership—of your business, your income, and your future—looks like.

Because at the end of the day?

The biggest risk isn't buying the wrong business. The biggest risk is staying stuck where you are.

It's time to take the leap.

A Vision for a New Future

I wish we lived in a world where every woman—and, for that matter, every parent—could build a life that feels *authentic and sustainable*, one where you can use your gifts, talents, and abilities not just to make a living, but to create a life that works for you. A world where financial security doesn't come at the expense of time with your children, and where career ambition doesn't have to mean choosing between success and sanity.

But the reality is, we don't live in that world—at least not yet.

We live in a system where profit and bottom lines are often valued more than holistic, balanced lives. Where traditional workplaces still expect you to be available at all hours, as if you don't have a family, and society expects you to raise children as if you don't have a job.

Can we work to change the way businesses and organizations operate? Absolutely. And we should. But for many of us, we can't afford to wait for that change to come.

We have families **now**. We need balance **now**. We need a path that lets us create **financial security and freedom** while also having the

time, space, and autonomy to parent in a way that is true to **who we are**.

That's what this book has been about.

This isn't just a career shift—it's an off-ramp from the exhaustion and frustration of trying to fit into a system that wasn't built for us. It's a new path, one that allows you to own your time, own your choices, and own your future.

Building a Better Future—One Business at a Time

Here's the thing: Every time one of us starts a business, buys a business, or invests in a business, we're not just creating more freedom for ourselves—we're changing the game for others.

We live in a world where **less than 2% of venture capital funding goes to women.**

Where women still don't have the protection of equal pay laws.

Where women-owned businesses still struggle to secure bank loans at the same rates as men.

Where the workplace was never designed to support working parents, caregivers, or women who want both ambition and balance.

But women business owners are rewriting these rules:

Chani, whose story you read earlier, built a business that pays every employee a minimum of $80,000 a year, plus full health, dental, and vision benefits. They have a flexible work-from-home policy, a four-day workweek, unlimited paid vacation, seven weeks of paid office closure, a stipend to help employees build wealth, and even unlimited menstrual leave.

Sybilla Mastersfund, a venture capital firm, invests only in startups with at least one female founder. They've created a completely hybrid work model, so employees can live and work from anywhere, and they close the entire company for August and December, recognizing that people need real time to reset and recharge.

Swella Beauty, a hair braiding business, doesn't just hire stylists—they create salon owners. Using a franchise model with affordable buy-in costs, they empower their stylists to go from employees to entrepreneurs. They're proving that financial freedom isn't just for those who start with wealth—it's for anyone willing to take the leap.

But it's not just these standout examples.

- **Women-owned businesses are growing at nearly twice the rate** of those owned by men.
- **They generate $1.8 trillion in revenue annually** in the U.S. alone.
- **They are more likely to create flexible, family-friendly workplaces**—because they know firsthand how much it matters.

And the ripple effect is real.

When women earn more, they reinvest more. Studies show that women reinvest **90% of their income into their families and communities** compared to 30–40% for men.

When women employ other women, they change workplace culture. They create environments where maternity leave isn't a liability, where flexible schedules don't kill careers, and where professional success doesn't mean sacrificing family life.

When women own businesses, they create new role models. Every time a mother, a daughter, a niece, or a friend sees someone they know building wealth on their own terms, the belief of what's possible shifts.

Maybe You'll Build the Next One!

Maybe you'll be the one to hire a woman re-entering the workforce after having a child.

Maybe you'll create the company that pays employees enough to actually build wealth.

Maybe you'll start a business that puts freedom, flexibility, and financial security in the hands of more women.

Because this isn't just about making money.

It's about changing lives—including your own.

Your Life, Your Terms

If you've made it to the end of this book, then you already feel the pull toward something different. You know that a better way is possible. You don't have to stay stuck in a system that isn't working for you.

You have a choice.

For too long, women have been told that financial security means following someone else's rules—working within a structure built for a world that never considered our needs in the first place.

But **what if the world looked different?**

What if more women owned businesses—not just to create wealth for themselves, but to build workplaces that actually worked for people?

What if financial security wasn't something we had to chase at the cost of our time, energy, and well-being—but something we created for ourselves, on our own terms?

Every time a woman starts, buys, or invests in a business, she is shifting that reality. She's not just building freedom for herself; she's expanding what's possible for her children, her employees, and every woman watching from the sidelines wondering if she can do it, too.

So the real question is:

What role do you want to play in this shift?

Maybe you'll build something new.

Maybe you'll buy something that already exists and make it better. Maybe you'll invest in businesses that align with your values, putting your money behind the kind of future you want to see.

No matter what path you choose, every small decision you make to create freedom for yourself is also a step toward changing the landscape for others.

And the best part?

You don't have to wait for change.
You can create it.
And it starts right now.

My Wish for You

Herman Hesse once wrote:

> "My story isn't sweet and harmonious like invented stories; it tastes of folly and bewilderment, of madness and dreams—like the lives of all people who no longer want to lie to themselves."

When I left the corporate world, I had no idea the twists and turns my life would take. Would it have been easier if I had stayed at the bank and put my kids in daycare? Maybe. Or, more likely, I would have faced a different set of challenges. The truth is, there's no one perfect path—only the one that's right for you.

My journey wasn't always easy, and neither will yours be. But if you've made it to this point in the book, I hope you now see that there is another way forward. That financial freedom and time freedom aren't just dreams—they are possibilities you can create.

I want this book to inspire you, but I also want you to know that hard moments will come. The path to designing a life that gives you both financial security and autonomy isn't always smooth.

But even in the hardest moments, there is a force working on your behalf.

Years ago, in a moment of exhaustion and doubt, I received an email from my former Kundalini yoga teacher, Guru Singh. He wrote about a dragonfly called the wandering glider—a creature that has set the record for the longest insect migration, traveling over 11,000 miles.

What makes this dragonfly unique is that it doesn't fly it glides on thermals at altitudes of 20,000 feet, feeding on aerial plankton along the way. It doesn't arrive at its destination exhausted and depleted—it arrives energetic and ready because it rides the winds that carry it forward.

When I read that, I cried.

I had spent so many years working, striving, and believing that sheer effort alone was the key to success. It's how I had always operated—the bootstrap kid from Philly who started working at fourteen; who got on a plane to Hong Kong without knowing a soul on the other end in search of something bigger, the woman who built a business while raising two kids, determined to carve out a life on her own terms.

But at some point, I started wondering: *Was I making it harder than it had to be? Could there be another way—one where I didn't* have to push so hard just to keep going?

I didn't have the answer at that moment, but I had a vision—a belief that I could find a way to arrive well-rested and well-fed, not drained and depleted. That I could create freedom and financial security without burning myself out in the process.

So, I got a tattoo of a dragonfly on my arm as a reminder. And now, whenever I feel myself slipping back into a frantic, fear-based push to make things happen, I look at it and remind myself:

There is another way.

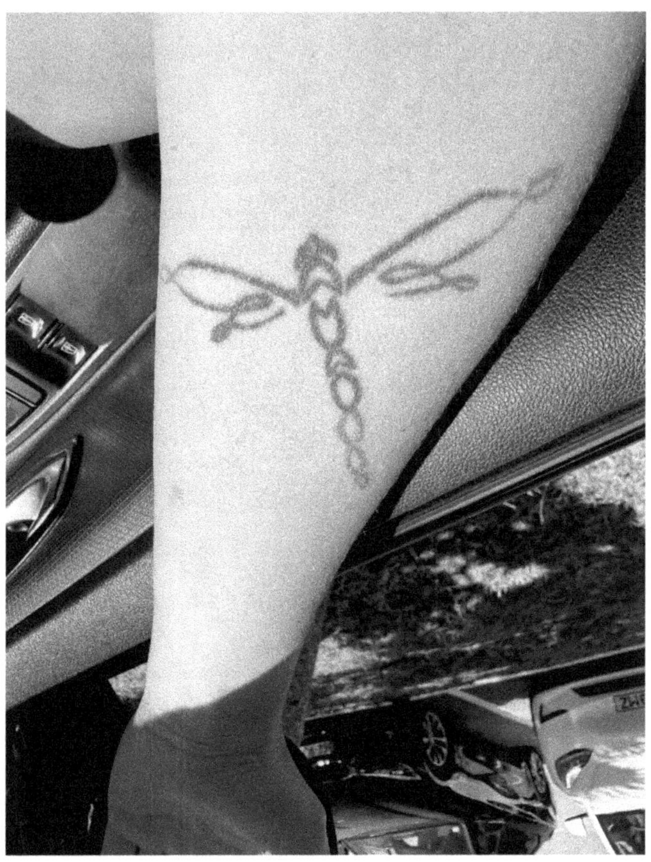

This Is My Wish for You

I don't know the exact reason you picked up this book. Maybe you're tired of feeling stretched between work and family. Maybe you want more freedom, more security, more time. Maybe you want to build a legacy that allows your kids to grow up watching their mother fully own her choices.

Whatever brought you here, my wish for you is this:

I don't want you to feel *trapped* between financial survival and the life you want.

I don't want you to feel *stuck* in a job that drains you.
I don't want you staying in an unfulfilling, dead or abusive relationship because you feel economically trapped.

I don't want you to feel like you have to choose between being there for your children and building wealth for your future.
I hope that, through this book, you've seen that you do have choices.

You can take control of your time.
You can build something that gives you both freedom and security.
And you can do it without burning yourself out in the process.

I also wish we lived in a world that didn't put women in these hard places to begin with. This isn't that world yet. But I believe we can change it—one woman, one family, one business at a time.

And until that time comes, always know this:

Regardless of what the world hands you, you can always make the choice to be free.

Glossary of Terms

A

Acquisition Entrepreneurship – The process of buying an existing business rather than starting one from scratch.

Amortization – The process of paying off debt in regular installments over time, which includes both principal and interest.

Asset – Anything of value that you own, such as real estate, businesses, stocks, or intellectual property.

B

Be the House – A concept in the book that encourages owning assets that generate income, rather than trading time for money, much like how a casino makes money by running the house rather than gambling.

Bootstrapping – Starting or growing a business with little to no external funding, relying instead on personal savings and business revenue.

Business Broker – A professional who helps buyers and sellers of businesses connect, negotiate, and complete transactions.

C

Cap Rate (Capitalization Rate) – A formula used to measure the return on a business or property investment, calculated as **NOI (Net Operating Income) ÷ Purchase Price**. A higher cap rate generally indicates a riskier investment.

Cash Flow – The money coming in and out of a business, determining whether it has enough liquidity to operate effectively.

Collateral – An asset pledged as security for a loan, which can be seized by the lender if the borrower fails to repay.

Creator/Artist (Inner Team Archetype) – One of the three key inner team archetypes from Deborah Price's money coaching framework, representing the part of you that uses talents, skills, and craftsmanship to create value.

D

Debt Coverage Ratio (DCR) – A financial metric used by lenders to determine if a business generates enough income to cover its debt obligations.

Due Diligence – The research and analysis done before purchasing a business to ensure its financial health, risks, and viability.

E

EBITDA (Earnings Before Interest, Taxes, Depreciation, and Amortization) – A measure of a business's profitability before certain expenses are deducted, giving a clearer picture of its financial health.

Equity – Ownership in a company or asset, representing the portion that belongs to the owner(s) after debts and liabilities are subtracted.

F

Freedom Baseline – The minimum amount of money needed to cover your essential expenses without being financially dependent on a traditional job.

Franchise – A business model where an individual (the franchisee) purchases the rights to operate a business using an established brand's systems, processes, and support.

I

Interest-Only Loan – A loan where the borrower only pays interest for a set period, keeping monthly payments lower before the principal starts being repaid.

Internal Team – The combination of the *Magician, Creator/Artist, and Warrior* archetypes that help drive business success.

Investment Income – Money earned from assets like stocks, rental properties, or business ownership rather than direct labor.

L

Leverage – Using borrowed money to increase potential returns on an investment.

Lifestyle Inflation – The tendency to increase spending as income rises, often preventing wealth accumulation.

M

Magician (Inner Team Archetype) – The visionary part of you that generates innovative business ideas and connects the dots in unexpected ways.

Mastermind Group – A peer group of business owners or professionals who share knowledge, accountability, and support.

Money Machine – A system of income-generating assets that provide financial security and freedom, reducing reliance on traditional employment.

N

Net Operating Income (NOI) – A key financial metric that represents a business's revenue after operating expenses are deducted but before taxes and interest are considered.

No-Spend Days – A savings strategy where you challenge yourself to go days or weeks without spending money on non-essentials.

O

Owner Financing (Seller Financing) – When the seller of a business agrees to finance part of the purchase price, allowing the buyer to pay over time instead of requiring all cash upfront.

P

Passive Income – Income that requires minimal effort to maintain, such as rental income, dividends, or business profits from a well-managed system.

Phinevo Test – A free online assessment (available at **www.phinevo. com**) that helps identify your dominant money archetypes and areas for growth.

R

Risk vs. Reward – The balance between potential gain and potential loss when making financial or business decisions.

ROI (Return on Investment) – A measure of how much profit is earned on an investment relative to its cost, calculated as (Net Profit ÷ Total Investment) × 100.

S

SBA Loan (Small Business Administration Loan) – A government-backed loan program designed to help entrepreneurs buy or start businesses with lower down payments and better terms.

Seller Note (Subordinated Loan) – A form of financing where the seller provides a loan to the buyer as part of the business purchase, typically interest-only for a set period.

Side Hustle – A business or gig done in addition to a full-time job to generate extra income.

Sweat Equity – The value of time and effort put into a business instead of cash investment.

<h1 style="text-align:center">T</h1>

Time Freedom – The ability to control your own schedule and prioritize life on your own terms, rather than being dictated by a job.

Trapped Money – Money tied up in assets that aren't generating income or providing financial security.

<h1 style="text-align:center">W</h1>

Warrior (Inner Team Archetype) – The action-taker, executor, and enforcer who gets things done and moves the business forward.

Wandering Glider (Dragonfly Metaphor) – A metaphor from the epilogue, symbolizing the ability to ride the winds of opportunity instead of struggling against them, arriving at your destination well-rested instead of exhausted.

Final Thoughts

This glossary serves as a quick reference to the concepts, strategies, and financial terms discussed throughout the book. As you move forward, these definitions will help you apply what you've learned, making it easier to step into business ownership, financial security, and time freedom with confidence.

Recommended Resources

These books provide deeper insights into the topics covered in this book—from financial freedom to business ownership, negotiation, and work-life balance.

INTRODUCTION

Freedom: The Real Wealth

📖 *Your Money or Your Life* by Vicki Robin & Joe Dominguez – A foundational book on shifting from earning to survive to earning for freedom, and redefining wealth as life energy rather than just income.

The Life I Didn't Know I Needed

📖 *Essentialism: The Disciplined Pursuit of Less* by Greg McKeown – A guide to focusing on what truly matters and designing a life with intention instead of obligation.

Moms Need Freedom and Safety

📖 *Invisible Women* by Caroline Criado Perez – Reveals how economic and workplace systems often fail to account for women's realities.

📖 *The Double X Economy* by Linda Scott – Explores the structural barriers women face and why financial security is central to autonomy.

SECTION I:
WHY A SEAT AT THE TABLE ISN'T GOOD ENOUGH

Chapter 1: What Women Want

📖 *Lean In* by Sheryl Sandberg – Examines the challenges women face in corporate environments and why traditional success paths don't always deliver fulfillment or freedom.

Chapter 2: How We Get Stuck

📖 *All the Single Ladies* by Rebecca Traister – Explores how social and economic structures shape women's personal and financial lives in ways we rarely question.

Chapter 3: Buckle Up, Buttercup: Changing How You Think About Money

📖 *Rich Dad Poor Dad* by Robert Kiyosaki – A mindset-shifting book that challenges traditional beliefs about work, assets, and how money actually grows.

SECTION II: THE BUSINESS FREEDOM SHIFT

Chapter 4: We All Need F-You Money —
Calculating Your Freedom Baseline

📖 *Financial Freedom* by Grant Sabatier – A practical guide to restructuring your financial life to prioritize choice over consumption.

📖 *The Automatic Millionaire* by David Bach – Shows how small, consistent financial habits build long-term freedom through automation.

Chapter 5: How to Make Money 101

📖 *The Millionaire Fastlane* by MJ DeMarco – A blunt challenge to the slow, job-based path to wealth and a call to build scalable income streams.

📖 *Company of One* by Paul Jarvis – Argues that small, intentional businesses can be both profitable and sustainable without constant growth.

Chapter 6: Savings Is Not a Four-Letter Word

📖 *The Index Card* by Helaine Olen & Harold Pollack – A simple, values-driven guide to saving, spending, and financial priorities in plain English.

📖 *The Year of Less* by Cait Flanders – A personal account of how simplifying spending and redefining "enough" creates freedom and margin.

Chapter 7: Money Flows — Income, Savings, and Debt

📖 *The Simple Path to Wealth* by JL Collins – A clear framework for directing income into savings and long-term financial independence.

📖 *I Will Teach You to Be Rich - Ramit Sethi*
A practical, no-shame guide to building automated systems for saving, spending, and investing, helping you take control of your money flow and use it intentionally rather than living paycheck to paycheck.

SECTION III: BUILDING YOUR OWN TABLE

Chapter 8: Rethinking Risk

📖 *The Intelligent Investor* by Benjamin Graham – A classic on margin of safety and disciplined, long-term decision-making.

📖 *The Psychology of Money* by Morgan Housel – Explores how fear, greed, and personal history shape our perception of risk.

Chapter 9: Choose Your Own Adventure

📖 *Rich Dad's Cashflow Quadrant* by Robert Kiyosaki – Introduces different paths to earning income and the freedom that comes from owning assets.

📖 *Your Next Five Moves* by Patrick Bet-David – A strategic guide to making bold financial and career decisions with long-term perspective.

📖 *The E-Myth Revisited* by Michael Gerber – Shows why systems and structure matter more than personal hustle in building a sustainable business.

Chapter 10: Be the House

📖 *The Millionaire Next Door* by Thomas J. Stanley & William D. Danko – Reveals how true wealth is built quietly through ownership, discipline, and long-term thinking.

📖 *Built to Sell* by John Warrillow – A guide to building a business with real value, not just a job with stress.

Chapter 11: The Advantage of Buying Cash Flow Up Front

📖 *Buy Then Build* by Walker Deibel – Makes the case for acquisition entrepreneurship as a faster, safer path to cash flow and freedom than starting from scratch.

SECTION IV:
YOU DON'T NEED AN MBA BUT YOU DO NEED SKILLS

Chapter 12: Why You Can't Buy a Million-Dollar Home But You Can Buy a Million-Dollar Business

📖 *HBR Guide to Buying a Small Business* by Richard Ruback & Royce Yudkoff – A rigorous, practical guide to analyzing and acquiring a business using smart financing.

Chapter 13: Finding the Right Opportunity — Analyzing Risk and Reward

📖 *Financial Intelligence for Entrepreneurs* by Karen Berman & Joe Knight – Teaches how to read financial statements and evaluate business performance.

📖 *Accounting Made Simple* by Mike Piper – A plain-English guide to cash flow, profitability, and basic financial literacy.

Chapter 14: The Inner and Outer Work of Building a Business

📖 *Money Magic* by Deborah L. Price – Explores money archetypes, self-sabotage, and the emotional patterns that shape financial decisions.

📖 *Who Not How* by Dan Sullivan – Emphasizes building teams and support instead of trying to do everything yourself.

Chapter 15: Buying Right — How to Structure and Negotiate a Smart Deal

📖 *Never Split the Difference* by Chris Voss – Tactical negotiation strategies for structuring better deals without destroying trust.

CONCLUSION: A VISION FOR A NEW FUTURE

📖 *The Almanack of Naval Ravikant* by Eric Jorgenson – Reflections on wealth, happiness, and freedom as skills to be cultivated.

📖 *Dare to Lead* by Brené Brown – A powerful book on courage, integrity, and leading with authenticity.

EPILOGUE: MY WISH FOR YOU

📖 *The Top Five Regrets of the Dying* by Bronnie Ware – A reminder to live intentionally and not by inherited expectations.

📖 *The Art of Possibility* by Rosamund Stone Zander & Benjamin Zander – A book about shifting perspective and opening new paths in life and work.

📖 **Small Business Development Centers (SBDCs)** – Free business mentoring and coaching: **www.sba.gov/local-assistance/sbdc**

📖 **SCORE Mentors** – Free one-on-one mentoring for small business owners: **www.score.org**

📖 **Women's Business Centers (WBCs)** – Free resources for female entrepreneurs: **www.sba.gov/local-assistance/wbc**

📖 **Phinevo Test** – Free money archetype test to understand your strengths and weaknesses: **www.phinevo.com**

FINAL THOUGHTS

This book is just the **starting point**. Use these resources to **keep learning, taking action, and creating the freedom you deserve.**

Acknowledgements

Writing a book is like giving birth—and yes, it's every bit as long, hard, painful, and humbling as becoming a mom for the first time.

This baby, luckily, had a fabulous midwife: my writing coach, **Jamie Morris**, without whom it might have been stillborn. Like any good midwife, she sometimes had to push the baby back in, turn its head around, and make me do things I really, really didn't want to do. But it was her coaching, patience, and fierce commitment that ultimately got this child into the world.

Having had two natural childbirths, I'll also insist that every woman needs a doula. While the midwife focuses on bringing a healthy child into the world, the doula's only job is to take care of the mama through the painful process. That doula—and quintessential cheerleader—was **Charmaine**. Her unbridled enthusiasm and belief in this project were invaluable. She pre-read sections, declared them brilliant and inspired, and told me to keep going even when I wanted to quit. Whether or not it was all true doesn't matter. We all need that person in our lives.

Lisa Fioresi walked into my first business as a guest while I was probably running around like a crazy person with a baby glued to my hip. She somehow saw past the chaos and became my ride-ordie BFF. She's been there through everything—the 2008 crash, the lawsuit, the fire, the divorce, Covid—and she's kept me laughing, grounded, and sane through it all.

My life, and the lives of my kids, have been graced by a fabulous group of staff who have come and gone over the years, each leaving an imprint on our hearts. To all who became family along the way—**Michele, Sonia, Denise, Karina, Martin, Wayan, Holly, Tufts and Felicitas**—thank you for showing up, often when life was messy, and helping me build something that mattered.

To **Michele Voss** and **Gillian Muessig**, whose belief in me—and financial support of this work—made it possible to bring *The Business of Freedom* to life. Your confidence in my vision gave me courage when I doubted myself and reminded me that what we build as women can ripple far beyond what we imagine.

To **Donna**, who served as editor, proofreader, spell-checker, and sounding board when I knew what I wanted to say but got tangled in the how—your patience and steady assistance were invaluable. You helped bring clarity and polish to these words and ensured that what I meant to say actually made it to the page.

To **Rica**, who designed the gorgeous cover and transformed this book into a beautiful visual experience. You captured its essence— the strength, freedom, and feminine courage at its core—and made it something that truly invites readers in.

To all the individuals whose stories added depth and wisdom to these pages—and who allowed me to share them so their experiences could inspire others—thank you. And to **Greg**, who told me from the very beginning that I had something to teach and share with the world, your encouragement was a quiet but steady force that helped me see this project through.

To the **Founders Circle and early readers**, who believed in this book before it even existed—thank you for your trust, your insights, and your willingness to walk beside me as I shaped this vision. Your support—both financial and emotional—brought this dream to life.

To **you, the reader**: thank you for choosing to spend your time and attention here. Thank you for your curiosity, your courage, and your commitment to creating freedom on your own terms. My greatest hope is that the stories and ideas in this book remind you that you are not alone on this path—and that the life you long for is not only possible, but waiting for you to claim it.

And finally, to **my kids**, to whom this book is dedicated. You were always my *why*—my north star and the heart behind my pursuit of freedom and presence in a world that doesn't make either easy. I'm sure there were moments you wished I had a "normal job," but at least your childhood wasn't boring. I love you both to the moon and back.